NEW ENGLAND'S UNEXPLAINED MYSTERIES

Ghosts, UFOs, Cryptids, & More

TONY URBAN

PACKANACK
p u b l i s h i n g

CONTENTS

"Normal people have no idea how beautiful the darkness is..."

INTRODUCTION

A note from the author

I've been fascinated by ghosts, aliens, and monsters from a young age. For me, it started with horror movies. In particular, *Friday the 13th,* which I watched at the house of some friends when I was around five or six years old. I was hooked on horror.

As the years passed, I read countless books about the paranormal, both fictional and true. I'd seek out local places that were supposedly haunted - old buildings, graveyards, you know the drill. When I was old enough to drive, I began to travel to famous (or is it *infamous?*) sites. The Amityville house, Lizzie Borden's home and grave, haunted plantations, the works...

I branched out into bigfoot hunting and watching the skies for UFOs. I visited parks where sasquatches had been seen. I drove along the highway where Betty and Barney Hill were abducted. I went to Point Pleasant, West Virginia, hoping to spot Mothman, but he didn't make an appearance.

Soon after I became a writer, people who had experienced unexplainable phenomena began reaching out to me to share their stories. Barely a week passed where someone didn't stop or contact me, desperate to tell me about something strange they'd seen or experienced. I could see the truth in their eyes, the fear in their faces. These people weren't pulling my leg. Many had been traumatized by what they had experienced, and they needed to be heard.

I wanted to help them share their stories. So I began conducting formal interviews. It might be easy to scoff from afar, but when you've sat across from people reliving some of the scariest moments of their lives, you quickly understand there are mysteries out there that go beyond explanation. We've always been led to believe that spirits and creatures that can't be found in textbooks don't exist, but after spending time with the people who have seen them, I believe they're all too real.

In this book, I've tried to recreate the stories of the men and women who experienced these strange events as accurately as possible and in their own words. That means preserving their natural cadence and not exaggerating for dramatic effect. I want to share their truth, and I hope you enjoy reading it.

Some of these women and men have used their real names, while others wanted to preserve their privacy and used pseudonyms or remained anonymous. I ask you to please respect their wishes and not bother them on social media or try to make contact with them. Just because they're sharing their experiences publicly doesn't mean they want to be public figures. Please respect their boundaries.

I hope you enjoy reading about these encounters as much as I enjoyed hearing them from the people who lived through them.

Happy reading,

Tony Urban

A KNOCK AT NIGHT

WITNESS: ERIN JOHNSON

LOCATION: Boston, Massachusetts

. . .

BEING a broke college student is no fun. Between classes and volleyball, I didn't have time for a *real* part-time job, so I started a side hustle watching dogs and house-sitting. It was a pretty great gig, not only because the money was good (really good actually), but it also got me out of the dorm and away from my roommate, who seemed to be majoring in partying with a minor in being a pain in my butt.

I'd always loved dogs, and getting to just chill with them after a day of classes, take them for walks, play with them, and so on was terrific. Most of my gigs were simple and forgettable, relaxing long weekends that also gave me spending money.

But my last job ruined everything.

A nice couple in Back Bay had heard about me through one of their friends. They were going out of town for Easter weekend and needed someone to stay with Morty, their chubby, little corgi. Yep, he was Morty the corgi.

I'd been planning on going home to visit my parents in Cleveland over Easter break, but those trips were always so hectic and rushed, and all of those hours on the road left me dragging. A job was a good excuse to stay in Boston and not bring down their wrath on me.

I met the couple (I'll just call them the Smiths) early on a Thursday afternoon. They were nice people, a little reserved, but I was used to that. The people who can afford to pay someone to *babysit* their pets are usually pretty well off. Plus, the Smiths were a good twenty, maybe thirty years older than me, so it's not like I expected us to be besties. But they were cordial and gave me a tour of the house, showing me where all of Morty's toys and food and treats were kept. Then they introduced me to the man himself.

By this point in my *career*, I'd probably watched in the neighborhood of forty dogs (and two cats). They all had their own unique personalities. Some jumped all over me and gave me kisses as soon as they met me. Some ran and hid. And everything in between.

Morty the corgi fit somewhere in between. He was seven years old, so he didn't have that crazy, frantic puppy energy, but he was a friendly little guy. He strutted up to me, his butt giving a little wiggle as he wagged his docked tail, then he rolled onto his side so that I could scratch his belly. I knew straight off that we were going to get along.

It wasn't long before the Smiths hit the road,

leaving Morty and me alone in the big house. Some people think strange houses are spooky, but I never did. To me, they were like my own personal AirBnBs. I put my suitcase in the guest bedroom and went back downstairs, where Morty was sitting by the door, probably wondering where his family had gone and why they hadn't taken him. Most dogs did this. There was an adjustment period of a few hours until they accepted that every bump or sound of tires wasn't mom or dad coming home and that they were stuck with me.

Morty was no different. He came around before too long, though, and settled in by my feet while I knitted a scarf. Despite being springtime, it was chilly, and I enjoyed the warmth he was throwing my way. Later, I made him his dinner and had a pizza delivered for myself. After we both ate, I took him for a walk around the block, and then, once we got home, we played fetch.

Morty and I settled into a comfortable routine, and we spent most of Friday in the cozy living room. Everything was going as expected, until Friday night.

After watching a scary movie (bad idea), I had a glass of wine and went to bed early, probably no later than nine. I was out almost as soon as my head hit the pillow. But that didn't last long.

Around two a.m. I woke up feeling like someone was watching me. At first, I tried to brush it off as my imagination, but the feeling only grew stronger as the night went on. I tossed and turned, unable to shake the feeling that someone was in the room with me. The Smiths had requested that Morty be in his crate overnight, and even though I knew I had locked the crate door, I thought maybe he'd escaped and was wandering around, causing this feeling of being watched.

I rolled out of bed, checking all of the corners and beside the furniture, looking for Morty. As expected, though, he wasn't there. I went down to the living room and found him sleeping soundly in his crate. I checked the latch, and it was indeed locked.

After scolding myself for being silly, I went back to the guest bedroom. Reassured that everything was okay, I climbed back into bed and covered myself up with the sheets.

Just as I was drifting off to sleep, I heard a knock on the front door of the house. My heart jumped, and I bolted upright in bed, trying to figure out who could possibly be knocking at such a late hour. I called out, "Who's there?" but there was no answer. Of course, there wasn't. I was on the second floor. There was no way anyone at street level could have heard my voice.

The knocking continued, growing louder and more insistent.

I threw off the covers and stumbled out of bed, my heart racing as I crept down the steps. As I approached the door, I hesitated for a moment, wondering if I should just stay put. But something compelled me to open the door. When I did, the stoop of the house was empty. I took a few steps outside, checking the front of the house. No one was around.

Then, as I stood there, shivering in my pajamas, I heard the knock again. And I realized that it was coming from *inside* the house.

I dashed back into the home and followed the sound of the knocking, my heart jackhammering in my chest, until I found myself standing in Mrs. Smith's craft room. That's where I saw the woman. But it wasn't Mrs. Smith.

This woman was semi-transparent, allowing me to see straight through her and out the window on the other side of the room. She was wearing a ratty old housecoat and had long, stringy hair. I would have thought some homeless woman had broken into the house if it wasn't for being to see through her.

And her eyes...

She was staring at me, her eyes glowing with a pale, otherworldly iridescence. Then, after giving me a long look, she turned toward the wall where a large painting of an old clapboard church was hung and started banging on the wall with both fists. This was the knocking sound I'd been hearing.

I gasped and stumbled backward, my hand flying to my mouth to stifle a scream. I could feel her presence all around me, cold and eerie. I wanted to get out of that room, out of that house, but my legs felt heavy and uncooperative.

I managed to turn away from her, but as soon as I did, the door slammed closed, trapping me inside. I fumbled with the knob, my hands shaking so badly that I couldn't get it to turn. I could feel the woman—the ghost of the woman— behind me, moving closer and closer. Her coldness washed over me like a fog, enveloping me.

With my teeth chattering, I closed my eyes and prayed that the knob would turn. And finally, it did. I jerked the door open and stumbled into the hall where I promptly lost my balance and fell into the wall on the other side.

As soon as I was out of the room, that heavy, frigid feeling vanished. The house was quiet and still. That sensation, that force I'd felt was gone. I held my breath as I glanced back into the room.

It was empty.

I blinked a few times, trying to clear my eyes, clear my head, in case I was blocking her out. But she was indeed gone. Nevertheless, I closed the door anyway. I would have locked it too if I'd had the key.

Even though the Smiths had said Morty liked sleeping in his crate, I couldn't bring myself to sleep alone, so I opened the door to the cage. He blinked at me a few times and sighed, like he couldn't understand why I was bothering him in the middle of the night. I cajoled him out with the help of some treats, then brought him to the guest bedroom with me.

I locked Morty and myself in the bedroom, lifted him up into the bed with me, and dragged the covers over both of our heads. But sleep was out of the question. Every time I closed my eyes, I saw the woman's ghastly face staring back at me, her irises glowing with some inhuman force.

No more knocking came, and the ghost didn't materialize in the room. As dawn broke, I climbed out of bed, completely exhausted, and tried to convince myself it was all some bad dream or figment of my imagination brought on by the junk food, wine, and scary movie.

But I knew better. I'd never been the type of person to freak out for no reason. I didn't have realistic nightmares. I was calm and level-headed to the point of being boring, according to most of my friends.

Around mid-morning, the Smiths called to see how Morty was doing. I told them he was good, which was true. The little guy seemed as cool and collected as ever. I couldn't say the same for myself, though, and maybe that had come through in my voice because Mr. Smith asked if *I* was okay. I said that I was and added that I was just tired. Then I blurted out—why I still don't know—that I'd been kept awake by a knocking sound.

There was a long pause. So long I thought the call had been dropped. Then he said, "Must have been the pipes. It's an old house."

That was a reasonable explanation, but it was a lie. I knew it, and he knew it. I could tell by his tone. He asked if I'd be okay staying there until they got home on Monday afternoon, and I promised I would be, even though I wasn't sure I would. But I'd agreed to take this job, and despite everything that had happened, I intended to keep my word.

I spent most of Saturday outside with Morty.

We walked around the block so many times I was surprised the poor guy's short little legs didn't fall right off. When we got back to the house, I threw the ball for him in the backyard. Anything I could think of to avoid being inside the house. But eventually, night came, and I had no other choice.

I took Morty to bed with me again, and to my surprise, I fell asleep in short order. Maybe it was exhaustion or maybe my mind just knew I needed a break, but all of the tossing and turning I'd expected to do never came to fruition. I was out for the count.

Until the knocking started again.

And that time, Morty heard it too. He started barking at the closed bedroom door, the fur on his neck all puffed up. His entire body was trembling. As scared as I was, I felt guilty. Maybe he was only scared because I had selfishly not tucked him away inside the safety of his crate. Maybe that was why the knocking bothered him on this night but not the night prior. I still feel bad about that, but I can't change it now, can I?

We stayed in bed, cowering together, all night long. I wasn't about to go down and see that woman again, and for some reason, I felt like I was safe in the bedroom. As if a ghost couldn't pass through a locked door or something.

The sound never came closer, but it also didn't

stop. Not until the sunlight began to spill through the windows. Only then were Morty and I finally granted a reprieve.

Even though I felt like a failure, I couldn't take it anymore. I called the Smiths and begged them to come home early. They reluctantly agreed, and I breathed a sigh of relief as I packed my bag and waited outside for them to arrive.

When they finally got home, they were shocked by how frazzled I looked. I told them everything that had happened, and they were sympathetic, but I could tell they were annoyed that their trip had been cut short. I told them they didn't need to pay me, and I think Mrs. Smith was eager to take me up on my offer as she stomped into the house.

But when she was gone, Mr. Smith pulled out his phone and Venmo'd my payment to me, along with an extra $100. He waited with me until my rideshare showed up. I kept apologizing, and he kept saying it was fine.

It got quiet between us, and for some reason, that made me uncomfortable enough to blurt out, "I'm not lying to you." He glanced at me but wouldn't hold eye contact, looking at the ground instead. Then he said, "I believe you."

I asked him if he'd seen *her,* and he said no, but that the people who'd lived in the house before them were elderly. The wife had passed away, and the husband, not wanting to live alone, moved into one of those retirement centers. Mr. Smith told me that when they (the Smiths) moved into the house, there was a wedding portrait of that old couple hanging on the wall in what became Mrs. Smith's craft room. He said his wife had thrown it out and replaced it with the generic painting of the old church.

I felt a cold blast of air wash over me, and for a second, thought it was a ghostly presence, but it was really only a gust of wind, one strong enough to kick up some litter in the gutter. Mr. Smith used that as an excuse to go back inside.

I never spoke to them again. I did, however, try to find photos of the elderly couple who'd lived in the home prior to the Smiths, thinking that I'd see the ghostly woman who kept banging on the wall where her wedding portrait had once hung, but I didn't have any luck.

I had several calls and requests to pet sit afterward but turned them all down. I'm still grateful for Morty the Corgi keeping me company through those two terrifying nights, but my days of staying in strangers' houses are over.

A WALK IN THE WOODS

WITNESS: STEWART MCIVER

LOCATION: Acworth, New Hampshire

. . .

MY EXPERIENCE with the unknown began with a bad fall. I was carrying an armload of groceries up the stairs to my apartment when I stepped on one of the kids' toys and went down. As soon as I hit the ground, I knew that it wasn't a normal fall. My leg felt almost disconnected from the knee down, and I was sure I'd broken something. Turns out I hadn't, but I tore my ACL *and* MCL.

Recovery was... well, it would require some profanity to really get my point across, but let me just say it wasn't fun. Several months later, I was still getting my mobility back to normal, and my physical therapist told me the best thing I could do was walk. I did the treadmill thing for a while, but staring at the TVs in the gym grew boring quickly. Luckily (if anything about rehabbing a bad injury can be lucky), it was summertime, and the weather was nice, so I hit the back roads. I'd park somewhere that traffic was almost nonexistent, walk a mile or so away from my car, then walk back.

Almost every day, I chose a different spot. Mixing up the scenery kept my mind off the monotony of walking and the lingering pain in my knee. I made a point to observe the wildlife, which wasn't really all that wild. Squirrels, chipmunks, stray cats, rabbits. A few times, I saw deer, but as soon as they saw me, they made a mad dash for cover. Those things sure spook easily. Once, I saw a red fox. Cutest rascal around. I went back to that place a few times, hoping I'd see him again, but I never did.

It got to the point where I actually looked forward to the walks, or more accurately, what I might see. Each day was like a little adventure, or maybe a scavenger hunt. I bought a bird book and taught myself how to differentiate sparrows from finches—that sort of thing. I'd make note of the species of trees. I'd never considered myself an outdoorsman, but I began to feel comfortable out there in the wilderness, or what passes for the wilderness in rural USA anyway.

Everything changed one late August morning. I'd gotten an early start because I wanted to beat the heat and was on the road before 7 a.m. The spot I chose that day was on the hilly side. By that point, I was almost fully recovered, so slightly more challenging terrain wasn't as daunting. I was on my way up one of the steeper inclines, steep enough that I couldn't see what was on the other side from the bottom of the hill.

I was about halfway up when I got a whiff of the most noxious odor. I thought straight off that it was a skunk, and from the strength of the smell, I was sure it must be close because my nose was burning, and so were my eyes. I thought about turning around and heading back, but I had no clue where the bugger was. For all I knew, it was behind me, and since I wasn't even a quarter-mile into my walk, I decided to keep on trucking and hope for the best.

The smell didn't get any stronger. It stayed about the same as I neared the top of that little hill. I tried to peek over the top, half-expecting to see a black and white flattened critter smashed into the road, but I still couldn't see what laid ahead of me. I took a look back. My car was still in sight, so I knew I had to keep going if I wanted to get my steps in.

When I crested the hill, I didn't see anything out of the ordinary. At first. No dead skunk rotting in the morning sun. No live skunk waiting to unleash a squirt of stink in my direction. I figured I was in the clear, so I started the descent.

I was still being careful about where I planted my feet. A bad fall will do that to a person. So I was looking down as much as I was looking forward. As a result, I didn't see what was waiting for me ahead until I'd come to the clear bottom of the hill. When the ground flattened out, I took a good look ahead. That's when I saw it.

A big, furry heap was sticking out of a thicket of wild raspberries. My first thought, crazy as it was, was GRIZZLY! I froze, standing stiff as a statue until I came to my senses and realized there aren't grizzly bears in this area.

Any bears we do have are as black as coal.

So what the heck was I looking at?

I knew it couldn't be a deer either. The fur was much too coarse and long. My next thought was a dog, some overgrown mutt that was out foraging for whatever it could find. But I couldn't think of a breed of dog that big. Any notion I'd had of being an expert at identifying animals flew out the proverbial window because I couldn't imagine what was rummaging through those raspberries.

Now, maybe I'm not a smart man because a smart man would have turned tail and headed back to his car, but I was too curious to do that. I crouched down and grabbed a small rock, no bigger than an acorn, and lobbed it underhanded toward that big mess of fur.

The rock landed a few yards shy. The animal didn't react. So, I grabbed another rock, a piece of quartz about the size of a plump grape, and tossed it. I didn't make contact, but it landed closer, and when it rolled, it came within spitting distance of the thing.

That got its attention. I still half-expected to see a grizzly bear when it began to back out of the brush, even though I knew that was crazy. Turns out, what I did see was much crazier.

All that brown fur I'd seen, well, that was only a small part of the animal. Its hind end. I guess it must have been down on its knees, grazing on those berries until I came along like a fool and interrupted its breakfast. Once I had its attention, it stood up.

On two legs.

Just like a man.

But it wasn't a man at all. Its back was to me, and it must have stood seven feet tall. It was as bulky as a Patriots lineman all padded up. I'm no hunter, so I wouldn't even hazard a guess as to the weight, but let me assure you, *huge* is an understatement. It was gigantic. Dare I even say, monstrous.

I never watched those TV shows about bigfoot. The closest I ever came were the Jack's Links beef jerky commercials. I never believed in sasquatch.

Until I saw one in person.

The creature slowly turned toward me. Not all the way, just twisting at its waist. Its chest, like its back, was covered in dark brown fur, and it appeared to be matted and clumpy in spots. Its arms hung down past its waist, almost halfway to its knees. Its legs were as thick as tree trunks, and even with the fur, I could see how muscular this creature was.

As that thing looked at me, I was so terrified I couldn't move. Couldn't even breathe. There I was, staring at something I didn't believe was real, something I thought was completely made up. But there it was, staring back at me. Making eye contact with me!

I got about a three-second look at its face, but those three seconds felt like they lasted an hour. Its head was mostly covered with fur except for the eyes. They were big and brown, and this might sound crazy, but they looked intelligent... As if they were thinking. They didn't look startled like a deer's eyes when you surprise one. Instead, they just looked back at me, calm as calm can be. No fear at all. Like it knew it was the superior being, and I was at its mercy.

Its mouth was hidden by its fur. So were its nose and ears. Its head seemed slightly pointed. Nothing dramatic but noticeable.

For the first time, I remembered that I had my cell phone in my pocket and reached for it. I had to get a picture because I knew no one would believe me otherwise. But as soon as I moved, the bigfoot gave a little snort. Nothing angry or threatening, but maybe a little annoyed. Then, before I could take out my phone, it walked into the raspberry bushes and got lost in the foliage.

I thought about chasing after, but even I am not that dumb. Instead, I turned to retreat to my car, walking much faster than I had since my fall. I had only made it maybe ten yards up the hill when I felt a sharp pain in my back. It felt like I'd been stung by a hornet and reached back on instinct. But as I was trying to swat away what I thought was a bee, I heard a little clattering sound against the road.

I looked down to see what had made the noise. Lying there at my feet was that grape-sized piece of quartz. The same one I'd thrown at the bigfoot. I looked toward the raspberry bushes, straining to see the sasquatch, but it appeared to be gone.

Despite feeling like I was alone, all of the hair on my arms and neck was standing at full attention. I didn't realize it at first, but I was shaking too. I took a few backward steps until I hit a divot in the road and almost lost my balance. I guess that old knee injury trumped my fear of the creature, and I turned away from the bushes and continued toward my car.

I made it a few yards, five, maybe ten, when I heard branches breaking in the woodline to my left.

The side where the bigfoot had disappeared into. I could tell by the sound that something heavy and massive was pushing through the thicket. And even though I couldn't see it, I knew it was the sasquatch.

I risked breaking into a light jog, moving as fast as I dared, but the creature was catching up to me. Gaining on me. I ran—actually ran—a few steps, but no matter how fast I moved, I wasn't going to win a footrace with it. It kept coming.

I reached the top of the hill, out of breath, my knee on fire. I could see my car in the distance. Safety, or what I assumed was safety, was so close. But the branches kept breaking. It was close, so close. The smell was back too. The air reeked of it; rotten eggs and wet dogs.

I couldn't run downhill without falling. I knew that as sure as I knew my own name. And even if I could, the creature would still be able to catch me if it wanted to. Catch me and do God knows what.

All I could think to do was shout at it. I remembered being told that screaming at a bear was sometimes enough to startle it. Even though this was indeed no bear, I had no other options.

So I shouted. Or, more accurately, I screamed. If anyone had been close enough to hear me, they'd likely have thought some guy was getting murdered. I never made a noise like that before or have since.

As the echoes of my scream died off, I realized the sounds of breaking branches as it chased me had ceased. The smell was still there, though, hanging in the air as thick as the mist of the ocean. I thought maybe I was onto something, and I shouted, "Get out of here!" Then I waited.

There was no noise. No sound at all. It was like someone had hit the mute button on the entire forest. All I could hear was my own panicked breathing.

I felt like this was my (only?) chance. I headed down the hill as quickly as I could safely move and didn't stop until I hit the flat ground. By then, the smell had faded and was barely noticeable.

The sasquatch had stopped pursuing me.

Once I made it back to my car, I sat behind the wheel for a good fifteen minutes, collecting myself and calming my nerves. After I'd recovered, I drove to the spot where I'd initially seen the creature. Sitting behind the wheel, encased in steel and glass, makes a man feel more impervious than he is. I figured the chances it would still be around were slim to none as I scanned the brush, and I was right. It was long gone.

All that was left was a bunch of smashed-down bushes.

And the stench.

I went back to that spot the next day. And the next. And the next. It's been a few years now, but I still go back sometimes, always with my phone in hand, hoping that one of these days, I'll see it again.

But now I always stay inside my car.

GHOST SHIP

Witness: D. Winters

.   .   .

Location: Atlantic ocean east of Block Island, Rhode Island

I'D BEEN DATING Chip for almost two months when he came to me with a proposal. "Let's spend the weekend on my sailboat." I swallowed hard and tried to smile. The excitement on his face was obvious, and I didn't want to crush his good cheer, but the idea scared the heck out of me.

Don't get me wrong, it had nothing to do with Chip. He was a great guy, caring and sensitive, but also confident and charismatic. However, he lived a lifestyle I had trouble relating to. One with private clubs, expensive wine, and fancy food I couldn't even pronounce. And boats, of course. Private boats that probably cost more than I'd make in five years of working in my boring, middle management job.

The only boat I'd ever been on was the ferry to Martha's Vineyard. Even that was a one-time thing, a summer vacation with my grandparents back when I was ten. I didn't remember a whole lot about it aside from it feeling like it had taken forever. But the ferry was big. Huge, to my ten-year-old old eyes, really. Its size made it seem safe and impervious.

A sailboat? Out on the ocean? Maybe I had

watched *Titanic* too many times, but the idea had my stomach roiling.

"Sounds like fun," I said to Chip before I could stop myself. And even though I felt sick, the beaming smile he bestowed upon me, the one that showed his perfectly straight, perfectly white teeth, almost made me think it was the right decision. Almost.

I tried to keep my mind busy the next two days by picking out outfits and swimsuits. To not think about this small boat alone in the open water. I half succeeded. I wouldn't go as far as to say I was excited, but the idea of two days with Chip, just the two of us, in our own little world... It did have a certain appeal.

We sailed out of Billington Cove on a Friday afternoon. I think Chip could sense my nerves because he kept us close to the coast for most of that first day. He took me past Point Judith, pointing out the lighthouse, which I admit was interesting to see from that new vantage point. Then we sailed around Block Island.

It was nearing dusk, and by then, we were far enough from land that I could only make out the barest glimpses of light. Of civilization. Chip had prepared a lobster dinner, and we ate on deck. Surprisingly, my nerves had settled enough that I could actually enjoy the meal. The good company helped too, of course. I wasn't quite in love with him at that point, but I was on the precipice.

As night set in, we sat together on the deck for a while, snuggling close together to fend off the chill in the air. I have to admit, despite my apprehensions, there was something alluring about the rocking of the water and the sound of the gentle waves splashing against the boat. It would have been easy to imagine we were the last two people in the world.

We eventually went below deck, and I'll leave the rest to your imagination. I had fallen asleep beside Chip, but I woke up with a start when something crashed into the hull. I sat bolt upright in bed, feeling like my chest was in my throat. What if it was an iceberg, I thought with *Titanic*-induced trauma. Or a shark. I'd seen *Jaws* too, of course.

Chip was still fast, his tanned chest rising and falling with each slow breath. I thought about waking him but stopped myself. It was just a sound, after all. We were still floating. I'd heard nothing break or crack. For all I knew, noises like that happened all of the time, and I didn't want him thinking I was some nervous Nancy.

I sat there, listening, and eventually calmed down. But I couldn't go back to sleep because I had to pee. So, I headed to the bathroom and took care of that.

I was on my way back to bed when I heard a bell. *Ding, ding. Ding, ding.* It was faint, and I presumed far off, but my curiosity was piqued. I headed up the steps to the deck, then glanced out at the water.

At first, I didn't see anything. Just black water, black sky, and pinpoint stars. I turned, looking in the other direction (I still don't know port from starboard... sorry), and what I saw seemed so impossible that I blinked several times, certain it would vanish. But it didn't. It was there. It was real.

In the near distance, I'm guessing about fifty yards away, was an old-fashioned ship, the kind I'd only ever seen in bottles. It made me think of the Spanish Galleons in movies about Columbus or the pirate ships in *Pirates of the Caribbean*.

Initially, I thought that maybe it was a replica of some kind, the way people buy kits to make "new" versions of classic cars. But then I saw that its sails, massive and stretching high into the night sky, were tattered. The wind whipped through them, kicking up scraps of material that clawed like skeletal fingers in the air.

My attention now more focused, I examined the ship itself and realized it was semi-transparent, like looking through a painting on a glass window. It was there, I was certain, but not real. Or maybe, surreal.

It was a ghost ship.

If I could change one thing, I would have screamed for Chip or run back down the stairs, woken him from his sleep, and dragged him back onboard so he could see it too. So he could verify what I was seeing. But I was mesmerized.

The phantom vessel sailed on in the night, coming closer to Chip's sailboat, but never too close that I felt like we were in danger of colliding. The ring of the bell, *Ding, ding, Ding, ding,* grew louder.

When it was within maybe forty feet, I spotted men aboard that ship. They seemed to be going about their jobs, but their bodies were... Wispy, is the word that comes to mind. Or maybe blurry. They left trails behind when they moved. I could see the dead sailors on the deck of the ghost ship, and as they passed by, I realized they could see me too.

One of them raised his arm in a wave. Without thinking, I waved back. And with that, the ship sailed into the night, growing smaller and smaller on the horizon, until I couldn't see it any more.

Then, I felt hands on my shoulders. I jumped and nearly screamed, until I heard Chip's familiar voice. "I woke up, and you weren't there. Thought I'd better make sure you hadn't fallen overboard."

I turned back to him and leaned into his chest.

"Your heart is absolutely pounding," he said. "Are you okay?"

I said I was. I was on the verge of telling him what I'd seen, but I stopped myself. Would he think I was crazy? Would he write me off as some mad woman and never speak to me again? My instincts said he wasn't that kind of man, but in that moment, I didn't trust myself.

Years later, after we were married and on one of our many sailing adventures, I did tell him. And he believed me without question. He'd never seen anything like I described, and I've never seen it again in the years since. But on that night, it was there. It was real. A ghost ship sailing on for all eternity.

ANDY

WITNESS: ANONYMOUS

LOCATION: South Kingstown, Rhode Island

I'LL NEVER FORGET the day Andy died. It was a Wednesday in April, and I was in the middle of teaching my third period art class when the school principal came in to pull me out. I knew something was wrong as soon as I saw her face. She told me that Andy, one of my favorite students, had been hit and killed by a delivery truck on his way to school earlier that morning.

I couldn't believe it. Andy was only twelve years old, and he had his whole life ahead of him. He was always such a bright and curious student, eager to learn and participate in class. And a very gifted painter. I couldn't imagine a world without him.

The days that followed Andy's death were a blur. I couldn't focus on anything, and I found myself constantly thinking about him. I didn't want to go to work, but I knew that I had to. I couldn't let my other students down. But it was hard. Every time I walked into my classroom, I felt like Andy was still there, sitting at his desk, staring back at me.

As the weeks passed, I started to see glimpses of Andy everywhere. At first, I thought it was just my imagination playing tricks on me, but as the days went on, the sightings became more frequent and more vivid. I'd see him out of the corner of my eye, walking down the hallway or sitting in the back of my classroom. I tried to tell myself that my grief was making me see what I wanted to see, but deep down, I knew that it was something more.

Although I'd cared about Andy, seeing this—-I guess I have to use the word *ghost*—was scary. I couldn't shake off the feeling of dread and terror that washed over me every time I saw him.

Soon, it wasn't happening just at the school. I'd see Andy on the sidewalks, in the store. Once, even in church. It got to the point that I couldn't sleep at night, and I found myself constantly checking over my shoulder, expecting him to be there. I started to wonder if I was losing my mind.

After a few months of this, I couldn't take it anymore. I had to know if it was real or not. One day, I decided to get proof. At school, I kept my phone open to the camera app and kept it in my hand all day, waiting. I was determined to get a picture. But by the time the afternoon had rolled around, I still hadn't seen Andy's ghost. Maybe I was going crazy after all.

Then, just before my last class of the day, I saw him staring at me through the window of the art supply closet, where we keep all of the extra paint, canvases, and so on. I crept toward the door, raised my phone, and started to press the screen when...

The phone shut off. I hurriedly tried to power it

back on, but by the time it had loaded again, Andy was gone. Or so I thought. As I turned and walked back to my desk, feeling quite defeated, I heard a laugh. Andy's laugh.

It gave me goosebumps, but something about hearing his distinctive laugh made me all of the fear and dread I'd been feeling dissipate. And I remembered the kind, curious boy who'd been so eager to please me and be a good student.

Later, after the dismissal bell rang, I gathered my things together and was about to leave the room when an idea came to me. Certain that no student or staff member was going to walk in and surprise me, I decided to put my idea into motion.

I sifted through past projects and pulled out one of Andy's paintings. It wasn't his best work—he always took those home—but it was a nice water-color landscape featuring one of the lighthouses on Martha's Vineyard. A solid B.

Holding the painting in my hands, I decided to have a conversation with *Andy*

"Andy," I said, hearing the tremble in my own voice as I waited for a response. I don't really know why. I'd never heard any words from Andy's ghost before, but it just seemed natural to take a pause.

When no answer came, I continued, "I miss

your questions. I miss your excitement. I miss your talent and how seriously you took every assignment. But most of all, I miss you. You were one of my very best students, and I hope you know that."

The room was quiet aside from the low drone of the heat. There was no response from Andy.

"But even though I miss you, I want you to know that you can move on. You've graduated, in a way. And it's alright. You're okay. Nothing will ever hurt you again. A far better place than this is waiting for you."

A few more moments passed, and then I heard footsteps against the tile. They moved toward the room's exit, not quickly or slowly, just a normal walking pace. My head snapped in that direction, and I saw Andy's semi-opaque figure standing in the doorway, his back toward me.

"Andy?" I asked.

The figure slowly turned and looked at me. Andy's eyes were on me, and his cherubic face lit up with a smile.

"Goodbye," I said.

He raised one hand in a wave, then turned away and left the room. From the hallway, I heard his laugh one last time.

I knew then that Andy was gone, and that I

would never see him again. But somehow, that moment brought me a sense of peace. Andy knew how much I cared about him, and that was all that mattered.

DREADFUL DATE

WITNESS: JULIE MORIN

LOCATION: Barrington, New Hampshire

. . .

IT WAS SUPPOSED to be a perfect date night. After dinner and a movie, Danny and I decided to take a drive out to the countryside to enjoy some alone time. He parked his car near an old, abandoned farmhouse that probably hadn't been lived in for decades. The perfect place for some privacy. Then, we started to make out. We were teenagers, after all, and there wasn't much else to go in our small town.

We'd been dating for four months, pretty much an eternity when you're seventeen. We hadn't gone *all the way* yet, but I sensed it wasn't far off. I even thought that night might be *the* night. While I would have preferred more romance, or at least a more comfortable spot than the back seat of Danny's Pontiac, complaining never even crossed my mind. I was in love, and you know how that goes.

We'd been there for about fifteen minutes. Long enough to turn the windows opaque with steam. It was getting pretty intense, so when I heard a soft, feminine moan, I initially thought it had come from myself and that I was so caught up in the moment that I didn't even realize.

But then Danny pulled his lips away from my neck and asked, "Did you hear that?"

I told him I had, and we both paused, listening. But a full minute passed without anything else. I swiped at the glass, wiping away the condensation and peering out into the night. But between the smeary remnants and the darkness, I couldn't see anything. Heck, I could barely even make out the farmhouse.

Danny, apparently satisfied that nothing was amiss, took me by the waist and leaned into me, kissing me with so much passion that it took my breath away. To say I was excited is a massive understatement, and I was eager to go along.

We'd gotten to the point where Danny had my shirt pushed over my bra, and I was working at his belt when we both heard a thud against the hood of the car. Danny and I both froze. Well, we stopped making out. I was busy pulling my shirt down before some town cop out on patrol could sneak a peek.

Danny crawled between the seats and hit the lever to turn on the headlights. The area around the car lit up in a haze, but we still couldn't see because the windows were steamed up on the inside. He grabbed the crank on the door and started to roll down the driver's side window.

I asked what he was doing, and he told me he wanted to see who was out there. It seemed pretty obvious after he'd said it, of course. The night air rushed into the car and gave me goosebumps. Well, I'll blame it on the cool air anyway. After all, I wasn't scared, haha.

Danny leaned out the now open window, craning his head side to side.

"What do you see?" I asked.

"Nothing," he answered.

"Well, we both heard something," I said. Then, I guess to prove I wasn't scared, I opened the door and scanned the area around us. For the longest time, I didn't see anything at all. But then, all of a sudden, reflected against the headlights, I saw a large, black shape.

I must have gasped because Danny asked what was wrong. I jerked the car door closed and pointed through the windshield. "I saw... something," I muttered.

"What did you see?"

It was a good question, but I didn't have a good answer because I had no idea what it was. I told him as much, and then, like a good boyfriend, he threw open his door and stepped out of the car, ever my protector.

I lost sight of him as he stepped toward the front of the car, and I didn't like that at all. I opened the rear passenger door and hopped out, so anxious that I was holding my breath.

Fortunately, I could exhale quickly as I spotted Danny standing at the front of his car. After a second, I realized he was staring at the hood. I circled around to join him and see what he was looking at.

When I got to his side, I saw what had his attention. There was a muddy handprint on the car's hood. It stood out clearly against the gray paint and was impossible to mistake. I reached out, not to touch it but to put my hand near it to get an idea of the size. It was slightly smaller than my hand, the fingers shorter. Clearly, the print belonged to a woman or a child.

About that time, the wind kicked up, blowing across us and feeling more like a winter night than the pleasant spring evening we'd been enjoying. With the wind came a woman's voice that spoke a single word. "Daniel."

Danny and I looked at each other, shocked and bewildered. Neither said anything for a long moment, and then Danny broke into a wide grin. Confused, I asked him what he was smiling at.

"It's got to be Rhonda and Rich. They must have followed us," he said.

Rhonda was my best friend, and her boyfriend,

Rich, had become friends with Danny by association. Rich especially was a practical joker, an unfunny one most of the time, so Danny's assumption—that our friends had sneaked out here to scare us—made sense. In fact, it seemed like the only reasonable explanation.

Now that I could breathe easier, I had an idea of my own. "Let's scare the hell out of them."

Danny was on board. We pretended to get back into the car, making a point of slamming the doors and then turning off the headlights, sending the area into near complete darkness again. Then, we crept toward the source of Rhonda's voice, tiptoeing through the high, dewy grass, and weeds. Along the way, we passed by the farmhouse, which did look exceptionally ominous backlit by slivers of moonlight. But we were too excited about turning the tables on our friends to be spooked.

As we rounded the corner of the house, I saw the black shape again. Even though it was dark, with the idea of the prank in my mind, I could now easily imagine it being either Rich or Rhonda with a black sheet draped over themselves. It just seemed to be hanging out near the edge of the woods, and I had to bite my cheek so that I wouldn't laugh.

I poked Danny in the side, then pointed out the shape to him. He smirked and nodded, and we made a wide, arcing circle toward it. We were extra careful about where we stepped, not wanting to break a twig or rustle some fallen leaves and give ourselves away.

After what felt like forever, we were within five yards of the shape that we were certain was Rhonda or Rich. I kept scanning the area for the other, certain they were hiding nearby, but I didn't see them.

We continued forward, both of us fighting off laughter. Then, when we were in arm's reach, Danny dove forward, grabbing with his arms, like a football player tackling the quarterback. At the same time, I screamed, "Gotcha!" and broke into an uncontrollable laughing fit.

Well, that stopped really quickly when Danny's tackle failed. He hit the black shape and fell right through it, crashing into the ground with a surprised grunt.

With that, the shape broke apart. It was like it disintegrated before my eyes, with black swirls floating off in random directions, and then vanishing.

"What the hell?" Danny asked as he crawled onto his knees, rubbing his forehead where he'd bruised it on a rock when he landed.

I couldn't respond. I was dumbstruck by what

I'd just seen. And then we both heard the voice again.

"Daniel."

It came from the forest.

"I'm gonna beat Rich's ass," Danny muttered as he pushed through the scrubby undergrowth and into the woods.

"Danny," I said, reaching for him and trying to pull him back. To stop him. But he was too far ahead of me to get a hold of him. All I could do was watch or follow.

I chose the latter.

We were probably twenty feet into the woods when I caught up to Danny. The only reason I was able to catch him though was because he'd stopped. He was staring at the ground, eyes locked on something. When I got to his side, he flinched and pulled away from me.

"What's wrong?" I asked.

He didn't answer, so I followed his gaze instead. Ahead of us, behind some rickety, knee-high wrought iron fencing were three old tombstones. Family burial plots aren't all that uncommon—I even remember some at my great-grandfather's property—but when you're not expecting to see them, especially in those circumstances, they made my hair stand on end.

But what *really* scared me was when I took a better look. Two of the markers were so old and weathered that I couldn't make out any names, but the third was still readable. Etched into the stone was:

"Daniel Pelletier. 1787-1804. Beloved Son."

Now, *my* Danny's last name isn't Pelletier—it's Morin—but the coincidence of the first name, along with the common age of seventeen, was enough for me to want to get far away from there and fast!

I took Danny by the shoulders and turned him around. He seemed to get the gist and grabbed my hand, and we hurried out of the woods, past the farmhouse, and back to our car. After jumping inside, I was certain the engine wouldn't start when Danny turned the key, but it did. The back end fishtailed in the dirt as he peeled out of there.

We didn't say a word to each other until we were back in town. There, under the light of the streetlamps, it felt safe. I told Danny about how the shape had broken apart and disappeared when he hit it, and we both agreed that we'd seen no evidence of Rich, Rhonda, or Rich's truck. Leaving the only explanation to be a ghost. I hadn't given any real thought to the subject matter prior to the night, but after what we'd experienced, what else could it be?

I asked Danny, "Do you think it was his mother?"

He just shrugged and said, "It said my name."

I reassured him that Danny or Daniel isn't the most unique name around, but for days afterward, I could tell he was unnerved and jumpy. Anxious.

Fortunately, what we experienced was no harbinger of doom. As time passed, we talked and thought about it less and less. We remained a couple, though, even through college, and we got married when we were twenty-five. We have three kids now, one of whom is almost as old as we were on that night.

Years later, I drove past that old farmhouse while running errands. It wasn't planned or even intentional, and I didn't quite realize where I was until I was almost on top of it. The house must have fallen in or been razed, and all that remained was the outline of the foundation. I slowed as I drove by, my eyes drawn to the woods. I didn't see any black shape on that day, but I didn't venture back into the woods to see if the tombstones still stood either. Not that I was scared or anything. Nope, not at all. Haha

FRIGHTENING FLIP

WITNESS: SAM ROTH

LOCATION: Pawtucket, Rhode Island

. . .

BACK WHEN HOUSE flipping took off, I decided to get in on the action. I'd worked in construction all of my life, so I felt comfortable with my experience level. I also had a nice nest egg saved up. It was to go toward my eventual retirement, but I figured, why let it ride in a mutual fund when I could double it over the course of a few months flipping a residence? I just needed to find the right house.

Most of what was coming on the market was out of my budget. I'd begun to think that I either needed to take out a loan or give up on my dream altogether when a sturdy, old duplex became available. The seller was only asking for fifty-five thousand, which gave me some breathing room for renovations and unforeseen issues.

I, like any good businessman, also decided to negotiate. I made an initial offer of forty-two thousand sight unseen, expecting to meet somewhere in the middle. To my surprise, the seller accepted straight off, with the only contingency being that we skip the home inspection. At that price, I figured it was worth the gamble. After signing all of the paperwork, I was given a deed and a set of keys, and I was in business.

The duplex had been built in the 1940s, but

had good bones, as the saying goes. The seller told me that it had been vacant for a little over four years. He'd bought the place intending for it to be a rental but never got around to fixing it up.

I wanted to turn it into a single family home, so I had a dumpster delivered and arrived ready for demo. As I stepped inside for the first time, I was overwhelmed by the smell of rot and body odor. I hadn't expected the place to smell like perfume, but I wasn't prepared for that. It even made me gag, and I was glad I'd skipped breakfast.

I couldn't understand it at first because the house seemed empty and clean. I'm talking, no furniture, no carpets, not even a folding chair left behind. Every room I checked was the same. Until I came to a small bedroom in the rear corner. I call it a bedroom, but it looked like a glorified walk-in closet. Maybe eight feet by ten feet at the max.

As soon as I opened the door to that room, the stench hit me like an uppercut. The source was obvious. In the center of the room was a grungy mattress that was probably white once upon a time but was stained yellow with urine and puke and God knows what else. Surrounding the mattress— filling the room, really—was trash. Food containers, beer bottles and cans, milk jugs, some of them half full and spoiled, fast food wrappers. Leftover scraps of food were everywhere and teeming with flies. It was vile.

I went straight back to my truck, grabbed gloves and trash bags, and went back inside to clean it out. It took me almost the entire day, and when I got to the bottom, I had to use a shovel. I don't even want to think about what some of that stuff was.

It was pretty obvious someone had been squatting in the house, or that room anyway, for a very long time. I suppose I was lucky that the whole duplex hadn't been trashed. Before I even started demo, I went to the hardware store and bought all new locks in case whoever had been calling that room home had a key. Then I checked and double-checked to ensure all of the windows were locked. Once that was finished, I was satisfied that the house was secure.

The first week went about as well as expected. There were some wiring issues that required hiring an electrician, but I won't bore you with the minutia. It was on day nine that things took a turn.

I'd been working since six AM, and it was almost eight in the evening. I'd stopped for a burger around midday, but aside from that, I'd worked straight through. I was exhausted but wanted to finish framing out a new entry to the kitchen before calling it a day.

I was about halfway finished when I heard the back door open and then slam shut. I was working alone, and I never used the back door. It had been locked since that very first day. So, the sound wasn't just unexpected, it was unwelcome. I'd been using a hammer, and I kept it in my hand as I moved toward the back of the house to investigate.

There were no overhead lights in the house, and no lamps either. I had a set of halogens on tripods, but those aren't exactly the kind of things you can carry around. I didn't even have my phone to use as a flashlight. I was pretty much walking into the dark.

I'm a big guy, six one and around two bills, most of the time. Between that and the framing hammer, I wasn't scared, but I wasn't seeking out a confrontation either. I wanted to give whoever had entered the house a chance to get out before it got to that point. So I called out, "This is private property, and I suggest you leave."

I listened carefully for footsteps but only heard my own breathing. "I have a hammer," I added.

Still, no response came. I gritted my teeth and continued forward. I was closing in on the back door when I heard a thud in that small bedroom, the one that had been wrecked when I bought the place.

I immediately felt angry because I believed the squatter had returned and was going to be a pain in my rump. I moved toward the bedroom and saw the door was closed. I'd kept it wide open so it could air out, so this was just more proof that someone was inside my house. Clutching the hammer so hard that my knuckles went white, I turned the knob and shoved the door inward.

There was just enough moonlight spilling through the lone window that I could mostly make out the walls and emptiness. But it was empty.

Apart from a large, human-shaped shadow in the back corner.

"Don't move," I said. "I'm calling the police." With that, I began to close the door, intending to lock it and lock the person inside until the cops showed up. But before I could even swing the door all the way shut, the shadow raced across the room and slammed into me.

To my shock and confusion, it didn't feel like getting hit by a person. I felt a force, but it was more of a pressure. Have you ever gone scuba diving or even dove to the bottom of a pretty deep pool? Well, it felt something like that. Like everything was closing in on me.

And then it was gone. Both the sensation and the shadow. I spun around, expecting to see someone running through the house, but there was no one. I went to the back door, expecting to find it had been kicked in, but it was closed. And it was still locked... from the inside.

I spent the next thirty minutes searching every inch of the house, from the attic to the basement before ultimately realizing I was alone. And with all of the doors and windows locked, the only explanation was that I'd always been alone.

I told myself I was just exhausted. Overworked and sleep-deprived. I figured, somehow, in that state, I'd imagined the whole thing.

After a good night's sleep, I went back the next day. Everything was still locked. Nothing was out of the ordinary. There was no sign of anyone having been in the house but me. Satisfied, I got back to work.

Over the next weeks, nothing extremely unusual happened, but there were small events. I'd be using my hammer in the living room, step away for a few minutes, then return to find it on the floor, instead of on the ladder where I'd left it sitting. Or, once, a box of screws that was on the kitchen counter got knocked off, spilling onto the floor when I was on the second floor. Like I said, small things. Nothing I could really point to and say, *This is certainly paranormal.*

A few weeks into the project, I had a plumber in to do some work that was too complicated to trust myself to do. He was working in the upstairs bathroom, and I was downstairs hanging a ceiling fan. I was perched on the top of the ladder when, above me, I heard a yelp. I paused, listening, and then I heard the plumber curse. I figured he'd just pinched his finger or banged his thumb. Typical enough on a construction site.

But a couple of minutes later, the plumber came down the steps, glowering at me, looking like he was ready to knock my block off. Before I could say anything, he grumbled, "You think you're some kind of comedian?" He used some blue language too, but I'll spare you that.

I asked him what he was talking about, and he said, "Don't act stupid. You threw water on me." As proof, he turned around and revealed that the back of his uniform shirt was drenched.

I told him I'd been downstairs the entire time and mentioned hearing him yelp and swear. He stared at me for a while, eyes narrowed like he was trying to get a read on me, to determine whether or not I was lying. I asked if he was sure it hadn't come from the shower or something, and he said that was impossible because he was on the other side of the room.

I guess I convinced him that it wasn't me, and when the plumber went to his van to change his shirt (I guess, when you do that job, you carry back up clothes), I walked upstairs to the bathroom. On the floor where he'd been working was a small puddle of what I assumed was water. But it wasn't water, or at least, not typical water. It was more like clear syrup, but not sticky. Just thick and gel-like. It was also cool to the touch. I grabbed some paper towels, wiped it up, and tried to put it out of my mind.

Within six weeks, I was close to having the house ready to go on the market. It was all finishing touches, staging furniture, etc. Nothing out of the ordinary had happened since the incident with the plumber, and in my ways, I'd moved on. I was just happy that the house was almost done, and I was (hopefully) in line for a nice profit.

I had a realtor in to do a walkthrough and take photos so that they could get it listed. She was doing her thing while I made myself busy. She was in the rear of the house, on the first floor, when I heard her say something, but I couldn't make out the words. I just figured she was talking to someone on her phone.

Then came her footsteps as she moved back through the house, toward where I was waiting. She looked a little frazzled and said, "Why didn't you tell me someone else was here?"

I told her no one was in the house but her and me, and she said, "Tell that to your guy in the bedroom."

She was annoyed, but I was just confused. I asked which bedroom, and she said it was the small one on the back, the one that had been trashed when I bought the place. I hurried back there—ran, really—jerking open the door and finding... nothing. The room was empty. I checked the back door, and it was still locked.

I returned to the realtor and told her no one was back there. She insisted there was and said she'd even gotten them in her picture. She held up her camera and was looking at the screen on the back when her brow scrunched up. "This doesn't make sense," she said.

I looked at the screen too, and it showed nothing but an empty bedroom. She told me that when she had the camera up and was taking the picture, a skinny, middle-aged man stepped in front of her just as she was pressing the button. She said she thought the man must be one of my workers and apologized to him before coming back out to me.

I didn't tell her about my own experience in

that room, or what had happened with the tools or the plumber. I guess I should have. To this day, she probably thinks she had imagined it. But I wanted to keep pretending that nothing odd was going on in that house. She hurriedly finished taking the rest of her photos, and we didn't bring it up again.

The house went on sale a little over a week later and sold for five thousand above my asking price just three days after. Sometimes, I wonder if the couple who bought it ever had any strange experiences of their own, but I've moved out of state and wouldn't even know how to get in contact with them. Or maybe...Maybe I'm afraid of what they'd say.

SIGHTING IN THE SKY

Witness: "Don"

. . .

Location: Open water near Nantucket. Massachusetts

When I was eight years old, my family went on a vacation to Florida. We flew from Boston to Miami, and as soon as that jet took off, I knew I wanted to become a pilot. I became obsessed with it, reading biographies on pilots, watching movies and documentaries, and even making model airplanes.

I considered enlisting in the Air Force, but after learning that the odds of ever flying as an enlisted man were virtually nil, I gave that a hard pass. Instead, I went for lessons at a regional airport and took all of the steps needed to get my pilot's license. Then, after years of saving up, I bought my very own plane. A very used (but well-cared for) Piper Cherokee 140. Not anything to brag about, really. But I tell you what, buying that plane made me feel like I'd *made it*.

I flew that plane for almost twenty years and never experienced anything more alarming than bad turbulence. That changed, though, on a pristine spring morning when I was flying out of the Chatham Municipal Airport on my way to the *Grey Lady*.

I'd made the trip dozens of times, sometimes taking friends or family to the island for vacations, but most of the time, I was flying solo and just enjoying the trip. Soaring over the open ocean, especially when you're alone, brings with it an incredible sense of peace and solitude. The rest of the world falls away with the land, and for all you know, you might be the last living person on the planet. But on that day, I definitely wasn't alone.

I wasn't in any hurry to get to Nantucket and was just cruising along and enjoying the ride when, to the east, I saw a glint of silver in the sky. At first, I thought it was a jet in the distance and didn't give it any thought. Then, within seconds, it was close enough for me to realize that it wasn't a jet. At least, not one like I'd ever seen before.

The object was less than a hundred yards from me. I'd been right about the color—it was silver. But it was oblong and pill-shaped. Later, I heard people describe these as looking like flying Tic Tacs, and that's spot on.

I altered course and flew in the general direction of it, still keeping enough distance to be safe, of course. But when I turned, it rocketed sideways. I'd seen thousands of planes and jets in my day, yet I'd never see anything move like that. One second it was flying straight ahead, as you'd expect, and the next it was moving at a ninety degree angle. It never turned or banked. It was instantaneous.

Within seconds, it was half a mile away, and my curiosity was higher than ever. As I flew toward it, I realized it wasn't moving. It was hovering. And it remained that way as I approached it. Once I was close enough, I could see that it seemed to be made of a reflective metal. It looked almost like chrome. There were no visible seams or windows. It was like one solid sheet had been molded into that form.

But that was impossible—or it should have been impossible—because the craft was far too large for that. It was longer than four 747-400s. At least a thousand feet. I could see no exhaust, nor could I hear any sounds of engines. Yet there it was, this silver behemoth in the sky, floating motionless.

I flew parallel to the object, straining to make out details in its mirror-like finish, but there were none to be seen. No rivets, no dings, no markings of any kind. I was nearing the end of it (no idea which was the rear or the front of the craft as they were identical in every way) when, without warning, it dropped.

It didn't tilt downward like a plane in a tailspin. It remained in a typical cruising position, just falling and falling and falling until... it hit the water.

I was high enough up that I can't say for certain, but I don't believe there was any splash. It was simply swallowed up by the ocean with no evidence left in its wake.

I descended as low as I could safely, all the while searching for wrecking, for evidence of any kind of its existence. But I saw nothing. I circled around and around—it must have been twenty times—but all to no avail.

I eventually returned to my main course, flying on to Nantucket. After landing, I saw the familiar faces of the men and women who worked at the airport and considered telling them what I'd seen, but I didn't dare. What if they thought I was crazy and reported me? What if my license was taken away?

Afterward, I made the flight to and from Nantucket even more frequently as I hoped to see the craft again, but I never did. Years passed without incident, and with time, even I started to wonder if I'd really seen what I thought I'd seen.

Then, one summer day in 2021, I was having lunch at the Crosswinds when a report began to play on one of the televisions. It was about Navy pilots who had become "whistleblowers" and admitted to seeing UFOs. One of the pilots referred to the object as a Tic Tac. When she said that, I choked on my soup.

An old pilot buddy of mine clapped me on the back, and I was able to breathe normally again. But I couldn't take my eyes off the TV. He realized what I was looking at and took the seat beside me. Then, in a low voice, he said, "I saw one of those myself. Must've been thirty years back."

I looked at him, trying to decide whether he was trying to get one over on me. I could tell by his expression that he was being honest, but I wasn't ready to share just yet. So, I said, "You did?" He nodded and told me it had happened on a flight up to Maine. The craft he described was identical to what I'd seen. But in his version, it didn't drop into the ocean. I had zigged and zagged in front of him and around him, and then disappeared over open water, further to the east.

Maybe he could see the look on my face because then he asked, "How about you? Ever see one?"

For the very first time ever, I unburdened myself of my story. He listened patiently, knowingly. Then he told me that we weren't the only ones. He personally knew eight other pilots who'd seen the same or similar crafts.

Did we all see UFOs? Technically, I would say

we did. Unidentified flying objects. None of us could certainly identify them. Were they being piloted by aliens? That, I can't say. But I've never seen anything man-made that looked and moved and behaved like that, and I'm quite certain I never will.

IT WAS THE PIGMAN

WITNESS: ANONYMOUS

LOCATION: Northfield, Vermont

. . .

I WAS a teenager in the 70s, which just happened to be around the time of the Pigman craze. Who is Pigman, you ask? Well, the way I heard it, it all started in 1971 when a farmer heard strange noises coming from his backyard. He went to the window to check it out, expecting to find a raccoon in his trash can, feasting on some rotting garbage. A pretty common situation in the country.

But when he flipped on the flood light, he saw a figure the size of an adult man, but one on the smaller side. About five and a half feet tall. The figure was covered in fine white fur and had the face of a man. As the light hit it, the creature let out a panicked squeal and scurried into the nearby forest. The farmer, in shock from what he'd witnessed, grabbed his shotgun and went outside. There, he found cloven hoof-prints in the mud. He followed the track to the treeline, but didn't dare go any further.

A few days later, a nearby high school was hosting a dance. Some students snuck outside to share a cigarette and probably an alcoholic beverage or two. As they were enjoying themselves, one of them heard a hard clicking against the pavement. The teens, assuming a teacher was about to bust them, spun toward the sound, only to discover the Pigman staring back at them. The creature had been approaching a nearby dumpster. The teens say he ran away, but most everyone believed it was the kids who ran first. Can't say as I blame them.

By the time I got my driver's license, it was 1978, and most of the paranoia had died down. The Pigman had become a boogeyman of sorts, a cautionary tale parents would tell their young children. "Don't go in the woods after dark or the Pigman will get you!" Or which young men would use to get their girlfriends to snuggle up extra close to them during a parking session. "Did you hear that noise? I think Pigman's out there." I might have used that last line myself a time or three.

But back to my story. It was 1978, and school was out for the summer. I'd been dating Kathy since the previous October, and we were pretty hot and heavy. Having my license and the freedom and privacy that it provided only accelerated things. Living in the country, there are lots of backroads on which to find some alone time, roads where the odds of a passing car are next to none.

A buddy of mine had told me about an abandoned farm along the Devil's Washbowl. I got it in my head that getting Kathy good, and scared would be the perfect way to... rev up her engine, so to speak. So, one night, I told her that the pigman originated on that farm. I said he was the result of inbreeding between a slow-witted farmhand and a prize sow. It was all made up, of course, and I think Kathy knew it, but she played along.

We drove out there a little before dusk. I wanted there to be enough daylight that we could explore the remnants of the farm without falling down an abandoned well or getting a foot caught up in barbed wire.

After parking in some weeds just off road, Kathy and I stepped into the overgrown grass and weeds and started exploring the property. All the while, she squeezed my hand so tight I can still feel the pain. But I liked it.

I told her I needed to take a leak and had to excuse myself. I could tell she was reluctant, but I squirmed and squeezed my thighs together, and she let me go. I moved about twenty feet away, dipping behind a falling down shed.

I didn't have to piss. That was just an excuse to move the next phase of my plan into action. I was going to wait there until Kathy came looking for me, then squeal like a pig and jump out at her. I knew she'd be furious, but they always say getting scared makes you horny, so it was a risk I was more than willing to take.

Well, my grand plan went to hell in a hurry when I heard some branches snapping to my right. I looked over, and let me tell you, it's a good thing my bladder was not full because if it had been, I'd have emptied it into my jeans.

Pushing through a big thicket of brush was a pale, chubby, figure that was almost as tall as me. At first glance, I could have believed it was a naked man, but I knew better. Then I saw the white hair all over its body. It made me think of peach fuzz, short and fine. It had arms and legs like a man. Hands like a man, too, but its fingers ended in thick claws. I couldn't see its feet amidst the brush. It had a fat potbelly and elongated nipples on its chest. For some reason, that last detail really sticks with me. So gross.

The face, though, that's even more burned into my memory. While the body had man-like shapes and proportions, its face and head were completely inhuman. Inhuman and all pig. Its stubby snout oozed snot. It had two yellow teeth that jutted up from its lower jaw like it had a severe underbite. Its eyes were glassy and black. The top of its head was bald aside from that white fuzz. On the sides of its skull were two gnarled and twisted ears. They looked like chewed-on beef jerky.

I think it saw me at the same time I saw it.

Those beady eyes grew wide, and I imagine mine did too. I stood there, frozen. Just staring at it. Then, the Pigman took a step toward me.

Whatever had been keeping me in place broke. I spun on my heels and absolutely sprinted the other direction. I never looked back. I just ran.

I saw Kathy and started babbling, telling her to get back to the car. She started to laugh. I think she thought I was trying to prank her, which, of course, I'd planned to do, but when I got close enough for her to see me good, she stopped laughing right quick.

I'd caught up to her at that point and grabbed her arm. Together we ran back to my car and dove inside. My hand was shaking so bad I could barely get the key in the ignition. As soon as I did, though, I cranked it and stomped on the gas. I didn't even look in the rear view as I sped away.

It wasn't until we got back to town that I had settled down enough to tell Kathy what I'd seen. I don't know if she believed me or not, and to be frank, I don't care. I know what I saw.

FAVOR FOR A FRIEND

WITNESS: NORMA B.

LOCATION: Portland, Maine

. . .

"Do you want to help me clean a haunted house?" Belinda asked me.

We'd been friends since grade school, forty-plus years. I never knew her to be a practical joker, so I asked her what on Earth she was talking about.

For some background, Belinda has a cleaning service. Think of it like Merry Maids, but without the franchise. She'd always had an entrepreneurial spirit and had been in business for herself for over ten years. She had a staff of four, not counting herself, and they serviced a few dozen houses altogether.

Bel explained that she'd been hired to do a "deep clean" on a house that was going to be put up for sale. The catch was that, according to local legend, the house was haunted. The other girls who worked for her were so superstitious that they refused to go inside, and according to Belinda, it would take two full days for her to clean it all by herself, and that would destroy her profit margin.

I wouldn't call myself a skeptic when it comes to the paranormal, but I wouldn't say I'm a believer either. I leave open the possibility of there being things—ghosts, spirits, whatever—out there, but I was never scared of them or expected to see them. So, it made sense why she'd ask me.

The next weekend, we rolled up in front of the house—which was really more like a small mansion —with a utility van filled with cleaning supplies, vacuums, mops, the works. I wasn't a professional cleaner by any stretch of the imagination, but I managed to keep my own house relatively spic and span, at least for the most part. Still, when I saw the size of the place, I was ready to turn and run the other direction.

As if sensing my mood, Bel said, "It won't be as bad as it looks. I promise."

I wasn't sure I believed her, but I'd agreed to help, so I stood by my word. I began unloading the van while Bel unlocked the house.

The first time I stepped inside, I sneezed. A layer of dust thick enough to write the alphabet coated everything. And I really mean everything. Tables, walls, the hardwood floors. The furniture— what there was of it—was all covered with old sheets. We removed those first, kicking up even more dust. Thank goodness neither of us had allergies!

The house had been sitting empty for over a decade. The owner, some little old man, had gone into a nursing home after having health issues, and the house hadn't seen a living soul since then. He'd died a few months ago, and some long-lost relative— I think it was a niece—inherited the property. But she lived in Colorado and just wanted the place sold off as fast as possible.

For sitting dormant for so long, I was surprised that the house was in such good shape. You could tell it had been well-built and no expenses had been spared. There was intricate woodworking and moulding framed in all of the doors and windows. The floors were solid oak. The ceilings must have been twelve-feet high. What furniture there was was high end, the type of stuff you'd pay a fortune for in an antique store.

Despite its size, and all of the dust, the house didn't feel intimidating in any way. There were no *bad vibes*, I guess you'd say. As we worked, I asked Bel where the idea that it was haunted had come from.

She sighed. "Do you really want to know?"

I assured her I did, and she gave me the story in broad strokes. Apparently, the little old man who'd lived there hadn't always been so little and old. Not one, but two of his wives had died inside the house under... let's just say, unusual circumstances. There was a lot of hot gossip around town that he'd murdered them both, but there was never enough evidence to charge him. Or, considering his vast wealth, perhaps he had greased the right palms to keep himself out of prison.

I asked Bel what she meant by *unusual circumstances*. With another sigh, she explained that wife number one had been found at the bottom of the staircase. Her husband said she'd been tripped up by one of their house cats, fallen all the way down, and broken her neck. But bruises on her neck looked vaguely like handprints. Wife number two had drowned in the bathtub. The theory was that she slipped while showering, cracked her head on the tub, and knocked herself unconscious before she went under the water. But more odd bruises on *her* neck made the story questionable at best.

Bel told me that workers for the man in the years after had spied one—or both—of his wives in various spots around the house. She also said that many people passing by had seen the women looking out from various windows, perpetually stuck inside the house where they'd died.

As ghost stories went, I didn't find it all that original. Yet, when Bel announced she was going to start cleaning the kitchen and asked me to work upstairs, I felt mildly uneasy about wandering off by myself. I did it, though, and didn't complain about it. Not a bit.

I started off in a room that I assume was an office. A large mahogany desk dominated the space, and two of the walls were lined with empty bookcases. There wasn't anything else in the room, aside from a large chair, so cleaning it wasn't very difficult. After that, I moved on to the upstairs bath. The master bath.

The sight of the large, clawfoot tub in that room gave me a little shiver. I wasn't sure then and still don't know if that's where wife number two had drowned. The house had four bathrooms, so it could have happened in any of them. Still, being the master bath, it seemed the most likely culprit.

The bathroom needed more work. All of the porcelain tiles were discolored and spotted with mildew, and hard water stains had the tub a bad mess. I got myself a workout and about used up my supply of elbow grease as I toiled away.

I was about two hours into cleaning the room when I felt a hand—an ice cold hand—grab the back of my neck and squeeze. I jerked and spun away so fast that the scrub brush I'd been using flew out of my hand, across the room, and shattered the mirror above the sink. Seven years of bad luck were headed my way, I suppose.

I was sure that I was going to find Bel standing behind me, laughing her damn fool head off, and believe me, I was prepared to give her a piece of my mind, but the room was empty. I poked my head into the hallway, thinking I'd catch her scurrying away like a scared rat, but the hall was empty too. In fact, I could hear Bel's footsteps downstairs, moving toward the staircase.

"Everything all right up there?" she called out.

"Yeah," I muttered, feeling a damn fool myself.

I didn't want her getting a laugh at my expense, so I wasn't about to tell her what I'd felt. Instead, I went to the mirror and started picking up the broken bits, careful not to slice open a finger. As I cleaned up the mess, I happened to catch my reflection in what was left of the mirror. And, on my neck, I saw a red mark. A red mark that looked like a handprint.

I was examining it when Bel came into the room, blabbering and asking what had happened. I lied, told her I'd spilled some water on the floor, slipped in it, and fell into the mirror. Not a bad fib for the spur of the moment, if I do say so myself.

"Did you hurt yourself?" Bel asked.

"Just my pride," I said, just wanting her to go and leave me alone.

But she didn't. She's too nosy for that. She came up to me and started giving me the once over, looking for slashers or gashes or whatever. Then her gaze fell on my throat. On the red marks.

"You hit your neck?" she asked.

I shrugged. "Maybe hit it on the sink when I slipped."

Her eyes narrowed. There was no way a sink, even the edge of one, could make that kind of mark. I knew it, and so did she. But she didn't press me about it.

"All right then," she said, then left me alone, moving back downstairs.

I still wasn't ready to admit that this was due to anything but my own imagination, so I refocused on cleaning and finished off the room in short order. Then I moved on to the next, and the next, and the next.

It was nearing on five when I finished with the upstairs. I bagged up all of the trash, gathered together all of my used-up rags and bottles, and hauled them to the top of the staircase. I had an armload as I started down the steps and was being extra careful about where I placed my feet. Last thing I needed was to end the day with a tumble.

I was about a third of the way down when I felt a cool breeze hit my back. It was like I had stepped in front of a box fan. Then, as soon as that happened, I felt hands—two of them this time—

wrap around my neck. They squeezed good and tight, cutting off my wind. I dropped everything I was carrying - it hit the steps with an awful clatter - and I grabbed at my neck, fully expecting to grab onto a pair of hands. Because I could FEEL them. They were so real. I could even feel the icy outlines of each finger.

But my own hands didn't catch a hold of anything. I just hit myself in the throat. But the other hands—oh, I may as well say it... the *ghost* hands—were still there squeezing, choking me. I began to see stars, and my lungs burned. I thought I'd pass out if it went on for another half minute.

Then, stirred by the commotion, Bel rushed out to see what the heck was going on. As soon as she came into view, the hands holding my neck and the pressure they'd been applying vanished.

I dropped like a stone but managed to catch onto the bannister before falling down all of the stairs. Small miracle, that was. Bel came running, her face full of panic. At that point, I'm sure she was wondering why she'd asked for my help. She asked the same questions, what happened, are you all right, and so on. I was too embarrassed and shaken to hold much of a conversation.

I told her to let me be and tried to compose myself. Then I picked up everything I'd dropped and retrieved the rest of the cleaning supplies from the second floor. I took the steps very slowly and cautiously, but nothing else occurred.

I helped Bel finish cleaning the ground floor, and once everything was finished, we were on our way. As we drove off, Bel kept stealing glances at me. I was afraid she was going to crash the van if she didn't stop, so I gave in and told her what had happened. She listened patiently, and when I finished, she simply said, "Well, I warned you the place was haunted."

I suppose I should have believed her the first time.

NOT A FISHING STORY

WITNESS: ANONYMOUS

LOCATION: Burlington, Vermont

. . .

I DIDN'T GROW up in Burlington—I was from a little town called Putney—but I went there for college back in the nineties. A lot of people ask me why I chose Burlington, and I don't have a great answer. I liked the small number of students, though. I didn't want to go somewhere with ten thousand kids crowding the campus. Plus, the idea of being close to Lake Champlain was appealing.

You see, I've been an avid fisherman since about the age of six. My grandad took me out with him all the time. Little ponds mostly, or a creek here and there. Occasionally, we'd drive over to Chesterfield and put our lines in Spofford Lake, but that was a rare occurrence. Grandad passed on when I was fifteen, but I never lost my love of fishing, even to this day.

At Burlington, on evenings when I didn't feel like studying, I'd grab my rod and reel and head over to Champlain and see what I could snag. About once a year, I'd even save up enough money to take an overnight chartered fishing tour. On one of those trips, I reeled in a thirty-three pound carp. That's no fishing story. It's God's honest truth.

On a lot of evenings, I'd be on the shore until a little after dark. Fishing is a lot like gambling. You just think, *one more cast, one more try,* always convinced the next time will be the jackpot. When you're out there, it's hard to stop.

In the autumn of my junior year, I'd had a bad day and failed an important exam. I was annoyed with myself because I knew I could do better, and annoyed with life in general. To clear my mind, I chose my go-to. I went fishing.

It was going on seven thirty or eight p.m. when I heard a heavy splash in the water. I shifted my attention toward the sound, squinting a little not because I needed to, but just out of habit. At first, I didn't see anything at all, and then, a bit to the west, I saw a large, black shape emerging from the lake.

At first glance, I thought it was a tree limb. It was long and narrow, sort of tapering down where it exited at the water, then expanding a bit at the end. I was on the verge of looking away, of returning my attention to fishing, when that black shape moved.

It pushed further out of the water in a way that reminded me of a construction crane rising into the air. Then, the fatter part at the end swiveled toward me. It was then that I realized I was looking at a sea monster. I was looking at *Champ*, the much bandied about unofficial mascot of Lake Champlain.

In all the time I'd spend at and on that lake, I'd

never seen anything that would have made me think it was Champ, not even for a split second. And, to be candid, I thought the whole story was a bunch of BS. Just made up stories to bring tourists to a part of the country few visit. I'd have bet my life that Champ was as fake as a three-dollar bill.

I'm really glad no one took me up on that bet.

As I stared, I still couldn't believe what I was seeing. It had to be a big tree branch or some weird litter. But then it began to raise its head further, and I saw the light reflect in its eyes.

The creature was fifty feet away from me max. Its skin had a slight, iridescent shimmer. It stayed above the water, looking at me, for a solid half minute, then slowly began to swim away. It cut through the water, leaving a churning current in its wake. Although I only saw part of its neck and head, judging by the way it displaced the water, it must have been massive. I've never seen anything like that before in person.

Within just a few seconds, it began to descend into the lake, sliding delicately beneath the surface. And then, it was gone.

I waited until the light of day had completely vanished, hoping it would reemerge, but it never did. I returned to Lake Champlain countless times over the next fourteen months, up until my graduation. I've gone back several more times since, fishing... and hoping. But, so far anyway, I've never seen the creature again.

Nonetheless, I know it was Champ that I saw that evening. Nothing will ever convince me otherwise. I also know that something that size could sink a boat without even making an effort. So, there are no more overnight charter tours in the cards for me. I'll never go out on the lake at night again.

HOTEL HAUNT

WITNESS: RETTA J.

LOCATION: Boston, Massachusetts

. . .

I'VE BEEN ADDICTED to ghost stories and all things horror since I was eight. The start of my obsession began when I watched *The Shining* during a sleepover at Carrie Landry's house. All of the other girls were screaming and crying and traumatized, but I was hooked!

A few summers ago, I talked my boyfriend, Charlie, into going on a horror-themed vacation tour. It took some convincing, but I won him over by promising to join him for a Red Sox game in Boston for the last stop. I have about as much interest in baseball as I do watching my father cut the lawn with scissors, but I figured it was a worthwhile trade.

I had a bucket list of places I wanted to see. We started out by heading east into Maine where we went to Bangor to see Stephen King's house. I wasn't expecting any ghosts there, but I thought maybe we'd get a glimpse of Sai King himself. Unfortunately, there was no sight of him, but we did get lots of pictures. The gates in front of his place are amazing, with spiders and gargoyles! One check on the bucket list.

Next, we traveled south to Portsmouth's Point of Graves Burial Ground where ghosts are supposed to touch and push visitors. Well, we walked around there for the better part of an hour with no luck.

Next up was my most anticipated destination. Salem, Mass. I'm sure I don't have to give you the backstory of the witch trials. I was certain that, if we were going to see a ghost, it would be in Salem. Well, an entire day of sightseeing later, we had made lots of memories and bought lots of souvenirs but didn't see a single spirit.

The next day, we drove down to Fall River to tour the legendary Lizzie Bordon House. Despite its reputation for being haunted, we didn't see anything unusual. We didn't even capture a single orb in any of our pictures.

We were on the last full day of our vacation, and I admit, I was a little bummed out. I think Charlie could tell, too, because he canceled our reservation at a crappy little Red Roof Inn and booked us a night in Boston's Omni Parker House Hotel, which was waaaaaaay outside of our budget. He's such a good boyfriend!

If you don't know, the Omni is said to be one of the inspirations for the Dolphin Hotel in Stephen King's novella *1408*. There's a room, 303, that is supposed to be crazy haunted, but it wasn't available during our stay. I didn't mind, though, as we did get a room on the third floor.

We went to the Red Sox game (they won, much to Charlie's delight) and had a nice meal out before returning to the hotel for the night. I kept waiting for shadow figures to appear or maybe the water to the bathtub turning on all by itself, but neither happened.

The trip had us pretty wiped out, and by the time eleven p.m. rolled around, we were both running on fumes. We put a movie on the TV and crawled into bed. I bet we were both fast asleep before the movie was even half over.

I woke up around three in the morning to the sound of a door closing. I noticed Charlie wasn't in bed, and when looking toward the bath, I saw the door was shut. Closing my eyes, I was on the verge of falling right back to sleep when I felt the mattress move.

It was just a slight shift. I'm sure I wouldn't have even noticed it if I'd been asleep. I rolled onto my side, blinking a few times, trying to clear my eyes of sleep as I reached for the lamp at the bedside. As I fumbled for the switch, I felt the bed move again.

That was enough for me. I jumped out of bed, ran across the room, and turned on the main room lights. About that time, Charlie shuffled out of the bathroom, squirting in the bright lights. He asked why I was up, and I told him what I'd felt.

Together, we walked over to the bed, and that's when we saw two indentations. There, on the mattress, were distinct handprints. Charlie smirked and said they were mine. He thought I was playing a joke. But I put my hands beside the prints, and we could easily see that the handprints were much larger than my own hands. Then, Charlie said maybe it was his from when he had gotten up. He compared his hand to them, but again, the size didn't match. The prints were smaller than Charlie's hands by almost a knuckle-length.

Nothing else happened that night, and we fell back asleep a little while later. We stopped at a few more places on our way home to Littleton but had no paranormal experiences. That was fine, though. I might not have had an official ghost sighting, but I definitely experienced something otherworldly in that hotel room.

SCARY SLEEPOVER

WITNESS: KAYLA

LOCATION: Epping, New Hampshire

. . .

WHEN YOU'RE fourteen years old and your only friend tells you her house is haunted, you have little choice but to believe her.

I was the *new kid* in school, and even though I'd been there for three months, I still struggled to fit it. The lone exception was Laura. I'd only been in school for about a week when Laura initiated a conversation, and we became fast friends.

Laura had a few other friends but not a lot. I got the feeling that she was something of an outcast herself. She and her parents lived in one of the poorer sections of town, and the other kids sometimes whispered about her, but who was I to judge?

Laura started coming over to my house after school and on weekends. We had several slumber parties, and yes, we called them parties, even though it was just the two of us. We'd get pizza and make popcorn and watch movies. We'd talk about boys and make crank phone calls and practice makeup on each other. Typical girl stuff.

As time passed, I began to find it a little odd that Laura never invited me to her house. I wondered if she was embarrassed because of where she lived. I never wanted her to think I'd judge her like the other kids, so one day, I told her I wanted to see her room.

Right away, I could see the trepidation on her face and in her eyes. I almost regretted asking because I could tell I'd made her uncomfortable. I began to change the subject, but then Laura said, "I'd take you to my house, but it's haunted."

At first, I thought she was kidding, but her face was dead serious. I asked her what she meant, and in my mind, I was thinking about ghosts in sheets making *Ohhhhh Ahhhhh* sounds and jumping out and shouting *Boo* when you passed by them.

But what she described sounded a lot creepier. She said she would hear the ghost at night, moving around, inside the walls. Sometimes, when she was in the basement getting something out of the deep freezer, she would feel it envelop her, which she described as an almost suffocating pressure.

Laura said that, once, when she was taking a bath, the ghost shoved her under the water and held her down. She said she had been choking and thought she was going to drown until her mother rushed into the room to see what was going on. When that happened, the force holding her under vanished.

Laura's parents didn't believe her, but I did. And I told her that I wanted to go to her house, and together, we'd stand up to the ghost. All of the apprehension she'd been battling vanished, and she broke into a wide smile. She gave me a hug and suggested we have a slumber party at her house that weekend. I agreed, but if I'd known what I was signing up for, I might have made a different decision.

In the days leading up to the weekend, I wasn't nervous or scared. I believed Laura's stories, but I still viewed ghosts as Saturday morning cartoon fodder. As harmless pranksters.

On Saturday afternoon, I rode my bike to Laura's house, went up to the door, and knocked. A few seconds later, Laura's mother, a thin, tired-looking woman, answered. She welcomed me inside and seemed absolutely delighted that I was there and that Laura had a friend who was visiting her house.

A few seconds later Laura bounded toward us. She grabbed my hand and dragged me to her room, which wasn't dissimilar to my own. Posters on the wall, stuffed animals on the bed, glitter everywhere. The only big difference was that she didn't have a TV in her room, but that was fine.

As she showed me her toys and clothes and things, we gossiped about our classmates and complained about teachers. A short while later,

Laura's mom came to the room to tell her that dinner was ready. She'd cooked homemade fried chicken and sides. She was an excellent cook, even better than my mom (sorry, mom!), and when it was finished, I was stuffed. Not too stuffed for ice cream later, though, of course.

The afternoon and evening passed without any sign of ghosts or spirits or malevolent forces. I still believed Laura, of course, but with each hour that went by without incident, any apprehensions I might have felt dwindled. Laura and I didn't bring up the subject either. We were just two kids being kids and having the time of our lives.

Even though Laura had a ten p.m. bedtime, her parents seemed so pleased that she was having a friend over that they allowed us to stay up as late as we wanted as long as we kept the noise down. We did that and were up past one before the sugar crash hit.

I'd brought my sleeping bag, and even though Laura said I could share her bed, or take it all for myself, I didn't want to come across as rude. So, I took the floor beside the bed.

I was used to sleeping with a nightlight—an old habit I'd never grown out of. On the other hand, Laura's room was pitch black, aside from the dim glow of a street lamp spilling in through the bedroom window. Because of that, or maybe it was just being in a foreign environment, it took me a little longer than usual to fall asleep. Laura was out before me, but eventually, I drifted off to her puffy snores.

A little while later—I don't know what time it was because there was no clock in the room—I woke up due to having to use the bathroom. I went there and back. When I returned to the room, I noticed that Laura's quilt, the one she'd covered herself with when lying down, was on the floor. I was still drowsy with sleep, though, and didn't give it much thought.

I crawled back into my sleeping bag and was almost asleep again when I felt a cool breeze bow across me. It wasn't a draft. It was strong enough to make my bangs flutter. Just seconds later, I felt something rustle the bottom of my sleeping bag, at my feet. If this had been in my house, I would have assumed it was one of our cats, but Laura's family didn't have any pets.

I began to sit up, to see what was touching me, but before I could even push myself onto my elbows, two invisible hands grabbed onto my shoulders. I know they were hands because I could feel the fingers gripping me, the nails clawing into my skin.

Immediately, I was wide awake. I tried to pull away, but whatever was holding me was far stronger. Much too strong for me to move away, to escape. It pushed me flat onto my back, and I could feel coldness wash over my body.

A foul stench filled my nostrils, like the breath of someone who hadn't brushed or flossed in years. I couldn't just smell it. I could feel the air. It was coming in steady, even intervals. The ghost, or whatever was pinning me to the floor, was exhaling into my face.

I tried to shout out for Laura or her parents, for anyone, but I couldn't make a sound. I couldn't move. I couldn't do anything but lay there, motionless. Helpless. I'd never been so scared and began to cry.

I don't know how long it lasted. It felt like hours but was probably no more than a few minutes. Then, as abruptly as it had all begun, the feeling of being held down and the cold all disappeared. I was free.

I pushed myself into a corner, pulled my knees to my chest, and sat there until the sun came up. When Laura awoke, I hurriedly laid down, not wanting her to realize I'd been sitting up. Or that I was scared.

After a breakfast that I could barely force

myself to peck at, I left. I avoided Laura for a few days, then realized I was hurting her feelings and that none of this was her fault. I ended up telling her everything, and she wasn't surprised.

The incident didn't harm our friendship in any way, but from that point on, all of the slumber parties took place at my house. Sometimes, Laura would tell me about more ghost encounters, but I didn't really want to hear them.

Her parents ended up moving a few years later when her dad got a new and better job. They stayed in the same town but bought a bigger house a few streets over. I don't know who bought their old house, but I often wonder if the ghost is still there.

A STORMY NIGHT

PRIOR TO THE INTERVIEW:

"I'm just two years from retiring from my job as a State Trooper. I want to talk about what happened, *but I want to keep my name out of it. I don't need anything jeopardizing my career."*

Interviewer: "I completely understand. I'll keep your name private."

WITNESS: Anonymous

LOCATION: Parsonsfield, Maine

I WAS DRIVING HOME from work, down a two-lane road in a heavily wooded area, when a sudden downpour hit. It came out of nowhere, dumping rain by the bucketful. Even putting my wipers on the fastest setting couldn't help me see the road ahead. It came on so quickly that I barely had time to slow down before I heard a loud thud coming from the front of my truck and felt my ride shudder from an impact.

I saw a blur of brown roll up over the hood of my pickup, then fall off to the side. Like any good Mainer, I'd had my share of close calls with deer, but in more than twenty years of driving, this was my first collision with one. I muttered some curse words and stared out into the torrential rain.

I needed to check out how much damage I'd done to my truck. I also needed to see if the deer needed to be put out of its misery. But I didn't want to get drenched, so I waited.

Four, maybe five minutes passed, and the rain slowed down to a normal amount. I was still going to get wet, but at least, it wouldn't be like *jumping into the deep end of the pool with all of my clothes on* wet.

I shut off the engine, threw open my door, and tucked my head into my shoulders in my best impression of a turtle as I circled around the front of the truck. Stomping through puddles deep enough to soak my boots, I got a good look at the carnage.

My bumper was completely smashed in on the passenger side, and the headlight and its housing on that side was smashed too. The fender had a dent the size of a basketball. And, cherry on top of the sundae, the hood had a nice wrinkle that hadn't been there before.

There was no sign of the deer. I should have been relieved I didn't need to put a slug between its eyes, but all the damage it had caused made that seem like a small victory. At first, I thought the only evidence of it was a smear of blood on the headlight plastic, blood that was quickly being washed away by the rain.

As I crouched down to make sure my tire wasn't punctured, I noticed a tuft of fur caught on the bumper. I pulled it off, thinking it looked darker and longer than deer hair. It was soaked, of course, but it felt exceptionally coarse, bordering on matted.

I brought it closer to my face to get a better look, but as soon as I did, the stench was so bad that it made my eyes water. I'd never smelled anything quite like it before. It reminded me of stagnant water combined with rotten eggs and feces. I threw the fur aside, wishing I'd never touched it. I rubbed my hand against the truck, using the rainwater to try and wash the smell away, but it didn't work very well.

I didn't have much time to think about it, though, before I heard a metallic *clunk,* and I saw a rock about the size of a bottle cap fall to the road. I looked behind myself, in the direction from which the rock had come.

At first, I didn't see anything, but as my eyes adjusted, I noticed a dark brown shape crouched between two trees. My mind immediately went back to the deer, making me assume that it was laying there, half-dead, waiting to either die from internal injuries I'd caused or for me to put it down.

I stood, shielding my eyes from the rain, which was slowing further with each passing minute. I tried to see if the deer was breathing or not, hoping it was not. I'm a hunter, have been all my life, but that doesn't mean I want an up close look at a dying creature either. I took a step toward it, and then in a flurry of movement and the sound of bushes breaking, the dark brown shape stood up.

The sight only lasted for a second, two at the most. But it was long enough for me to realize it was no deer. It was shaped like a gorilla, covered in dark fur, and about four and a half feet tall. It dove into the underbrush and vanished.

I stood there for a long spell, trying to connect the dots. This was a week before Halloween, and for some reason, I got it in my head that it could have been a kid in a monkey suit. What if he'd been out playing a prank, and I hit him?

I jerked open the passenger side door of my truck, opened the glove box, and grabbed my flashlight. I left the revolver I always kept in there behind. In hindsight, that was one of many mistakes I made that night.

I jogged to the edge of the road, to the spot

where that kid, or thing, had been. I saw evidence of its presence. Lots of broken branches and trampled weeds. But no sign of the kid. So, I pushed into the woods, shining my light from one side to the other, back and forth.

I was maybe ten yards into the trees, when another rock flew my way. But that one had better aim. It conked me on the forehead, and a little burst of pain was followed by a hot trickle. I reached up, wiping at the sore spot, and my fingers came away bloody.

It was a minor wound, no worse than getting pricked by a thorn, but it made me more convinced that some*one* was out there. "Are you hurt?" I called out. "Did I hit you with my truck?"

The rain had almost stopped at that point, and the woods carried that eerie silence that happens after a hard rain, before the bugs and birds and critters come out from hiding. But it wasn't completely quiet. I could hear breathing.

It was a low *huff, huff* sound that sort of reminded me of a dog when it's starting to get excited. I moved toward it, aiming my flashlight at where I thought it was coming from. There was a big jumble of bittersweet, and as the beam of light passed over it, I saw not one but two sets of eyes looking back.

The first was at that same four and a half to five feet level, but the second was much higher. The creature they belonged to was eight feet tall.

Suddenly, the brush was ripped to the side, and two beings that I can only now think of as sasquatches were revealed. The smaller was clearly injured. Its upper arm was bent at an awkward angle, and a shard of bone poked out from the flesh and fur. Dark red blood oozed from the wound. It was standing partially behind the larger creature in an almost protective stance.

The bigger sasquatch was absolutely massive in size. Its legs were as big around as the trunks of a good-sized tree. Its arms hung well below its waist, almost to its knees. Its chest was a full three feet across. And speaking of its chest, amongst its fur were—I'm quite certain of this—two breasts.

The larger animal grunted and huffed, taking a step in my direction. When I realized it was coming for me, all I could think of doing was run back to my truck and get out of there.

I spun, almost slipping in the mud, but managed to stay upright. Then I ran. Branches tore at my face, flaying my skin, but I didn't care because I could hear the animal coming after me. For every three steps of my own, it closed the distance in just one. No matter how fast I ran, it kept gaining on me. I was sure I was going to die in those woods.

The lights from my truck shined in the distance, getting closer, but I didn't want to allow myself to get my hopes up. I could sense it behind me. So close. I could smell it too. The awful, nauseating aroma of it made me want to retch.

I could see the edge of the trees, the road, my truck. I was so close. As I stepped onto the pavement, I didn't risk a look back. I didn't even circle around to the driver's side as I jumped into the passenger seat, crawled behind the wheel, and gunned the engine.

As I slammed the gas pedal to the floor, my rear wheels spun on the slick road, and for a minute, I thought the sasquatch was holding onto my truck. Holding me back. But then they caught traction, and I lurched forward, going as fast from zero to sixty as my old Ford could handle.

Only when I felt I was a safe distance away did I look in the rear view mirror. The road behind me was empty. But as I drove off, I heard a loud foreign roar, a sound like I'd never heard before or since.

Looking back, all I can assume was that I had hit the *baby* sasquatch with my truck and its mother had thrown the rocks at me to chase me off. To keep me away from its wounded cub (or whatever you'd call a baby squatch). But I didn't take the hint and went after them.

I don't know if the mother sasquatch would have killed me or if she was simply trying to scare me away. Maybe I don't want to know the answer.

WE KNOW WHAT WE SAW

PRIOR TO THE INTERVIEW:

"Considering what happened to us after our sighting, our privacy is very important to us. Can you guarantee our anonymity?"

Interviewer: "Yes. You have my word."

WITNESS: Anonymous married couple

LOCATION: White Mountains, New Hampshire

IN THE SPRING OF 2020, we were pretty much stuck in our home, just like most people. Lockdown sounded fun at first, especially since we'd only been married for eight months. It gave us plenty of private time that we hoped would help us get started on a family. It turns out, there are only so many *extra-curricular* activities you can partake in before even that becomes routine.

We also binged countless shows on Netflix, learned how to cook French cuisine, and read lots of books. But as the weeks passed, being inside the house all of the time wore us down.

At the time, we lived in Gorham, and we began taking drives in the countryside. Gas was cheap, and the scenery was pretty. Just being outside, in the fresh air, was invigorating. Over time, the drives became longer as we searched for new areas to see and explore.

One Wednesday afternoon in May, we drove to the White Mountains, hoping to see some wildlife. What we saw was something even more unforgettable.

The drive was pretty typical, and the area was practically deserted. We only passed maybe two other vehicles the entire time we were on the road. As we were heading toward one of the higher spots, we noticed a plume of smoke rising into the midday sky. It was extremely dark, not like the smoke from a campfire or bonfire. This was almost pure black, like someone was burning tires.

With the pristine view spoiled, we were annoyed enough that we decided to drive in the direction of the smoke to see if we could determine what was going on. We drove for around half an hour, sometimes turning wrong and moving away from the smoke, but eventually closing in on it.

We got to the point where we could smell it. It was a very acrid aroma, strong enough to burn our nasal passages. We could see it was billowing up from the forest and seemed to be fifty yards away at the most.

After some discussion, we decided to investigate. We parked in a small pull-off area and headed back into the woods. Quickly, the smell became almost overpowering, causing our eyes to water and sting. We'd never smelled any smoke quite like it. Mixed in with the smell of fire was a metallic or chemical odor. Something very pungent.

We debated turning back and calling 9-1-1, but it seemed like it would be an overreaction until we knew more. So we kept going forward, until the smoke grew so thick it was like trying to look through a dense, black, fog. We grabbed each other's hand so that we wouldn't get separated and lost.

Both of us started to hack and cough, and as soon as that happened, we heard branches breaking. Something was running, and it was moving toward us.

Before we could do the smart thing and dash back to our car, we caught a glimpse of a tall, slender figure. It was human-esque, but not clearly not human. It had pale gray-ish white skin and wore, from what we could see, a slate gray jumpsuit. Its face was turned away from us, but we could see its arms were unusually long and its fingers twice the length of a normal man.

It appeared to be injured, with black fluid oozing from the back of its head and staining its clothing. It walked with an awkward gait, sort of throwing its right leg forward as if it was sprained or in pain.

Then, the figure spun around, turning to face us. We only saw it for a fraction of a second, but we both saw that it had two large, almond-shaped eyes that were the size of lemons. There was no nose that we could see, and only a thin slit for a mouth. There was no hair on its head, which was long and slender and almost cylindrical in shape.

Before we could look better or see more details, it ran in the opposite direction, and we quickly lost sight of it in the smoke. Both of us were so startled that we couldn't decide what to do, whether to flee or chase it, so we just stood there, until the fumes from the smoke began to make us nauseous. Then, we retreated toward our car.

We didn't make it all the way back before we heard more footsteps. It sounded like dozens of them. They were coming from the road this time, heavy and determined. It sounded so loud, and for some reason, threatening, that we decided to hide behind a nearby boulder. But before we could get there, we were confronted by several soldiers in Army uniforms. According to the labels, they were from the National Guard. They all wore gas masks and carried rifles.

"What are you doing here?" one of them shouted at us, his voice muffled through the mask.

We stumbled over our words, trying to say we

were just out for a drive, when two of the men grabbed us and started half-pushing, half-dragging us toward the road. We were so startled, and scared, that we didn't even protest. We just allowed them to direct us back to our car.

Once there, the soldiers opened our front doors and pushed us into the vehicle. They didn't say a word to us, but they seemed frantic. It was clear that they wanted us gone, and protesting was not an option.

We noticed that the uniforms they were wearing looked brand new, like they were straight off the hanger from a costume shop. That, coupled with their aggressive demeanor, made us both extremely cautious.

"What's going on?" we asked.

"Wildfire," said the man who seemed to be in charge.

We started to correct him. "But we saw an—"

"You saw a first responder," the one in charge said. "Now get the hell out of here and don't stop driving until you get back to wherever you're from. It's not safe to be up here."

While this was going on, another of the soldiers was taking photographs of our car, our license plate, and us.

We agreed to obey their command, and all but

one of the men, the one in charge, returned to the forest. He stood there, watching us, until we turned the car around and drove away. All that time, he kept the rifle gripped so tightly his knuckles turned white.

We had made it probably five miles before we pulled onto the side of the road. Shaking, we talked about what we'd seen. Was it possible we'd actually seen someone in a mask or a helmet?

We both agreed that was not possible. Our details matched up perfectly. We hadn't seen a man. We'd both seen an alien. Agreeing that we weren't confused or mistaken, we resumed the drive home.

In the days following, we watched the news and read the papers nonstop. There was never a mention of anything amiss on the mountain, no plane crash, no reports of fires. After a week, we called the police station and asked them about the *fire* on the mountain. After a long pause, they said there was no fire. We gave them the date and time and told them about the National Guard being there. Then the line clicked and went dead.

In the weeks after, we both noticed black sedans and black vans with blacked out windows driving slowly past our house. None of them ever stopped, and maybe we were just being paranoid, but it unnerved us greatly.

A few months later, we decided we couldn't stay there any longer. We bought a place down in Tennessee, and we've been here ever since. We haven't told any of our new neighbors about what we saw in New Hampshire. Whenever the subject of aliens or UFOs comes up, we change the subject.

But we do spend a lot of time watching the skies. And we both shudder when a black vehicle with tinted windows drives past our new house.

GHOST IN THE GARDEN

WITNESS: MARGARET L.

. . .

LOCATION: Clarendon, Vermont

MY NAME IS MARGARET, and I live in a small cottage on the outskirts of Clarendon. I lived here for more than forty years, most of them with my husband, William.

We had no children or pets. It was just the two of us. I never minded it either. William was my soulmate, my confidante, and my best friend. He was my rock and my everything.

We'd spend our days at our jobs. He was a school teacher, and I worked for the post office. After work, we'd enjoy meals together, a little TV, and work on our puzzles.

During the warmer months of the year, we spent most of our free time in our garden. He always told me I was born with two green thumbs, and most years, our harvest was so plentiful that we ended up with so many cucumbers and tomatoes and zucchini that we kept several neighbors stocked up on their veggies.

It was a good life.

Or it was until William died. His passing was sudden. One autumn day, he'd been walking to work when a freak accident ended his life.

I struggled mightily to come to terms with his loss and tried to carry on with life as best I could. But it was never the same without him. I was lost, alone, and brokenhearted.

The following winter was long and lonely. I almost decided to forgo our garden. I couldn't imagine tending to it without William at my side. But when March rolled around, I found some seeds we'd saved, tucked away in a drawer. Maybe I was grasping at straws, but I took it as a sign. I prepared the seeds for germination, tended to the young plants, and after the last frost, planted the garden.

One day in early July, as I was tending to our vegetable garden, I saw movement in my peripheral vision. I turned around, and there he was— William's ghost—standing right in front of me. At first, I thought I'd finally gone and lost my mind. I rubbed my eyes, fully expecting him to be gone when I looked back. But when I did, he was still there.

He looked just like he had in life, so healthy and robust. I felt my heart racing as I looked at him, not knowing what to do or say. As my mind spun, all I could get out was his name. "William?"

He spoke to me, his voice barely above a whisper, and said, "Who else would I be?"

As tears streamed down my face, William

reached out to me to wipe them away. I couldn't feel his touch, not exactly. And his fingers didn't displace my tears. But I could feel his warmth. It spread through me, just as if he was still with me, even though he was no longer alive.

I tried to grab him, to hold him, but my arms passed through his ethereal form. I stumbled forward a step, falling through him. When I turned around, he wore a wide, warm and amused smile. I told him I wanted to touch him again, to hold him, but as I spoke, he began to fade. I could see through him, see our garden on the other side.

He brought his hand to his chest, to his heart, and held it there. It was a silent gesture we'd shared so often during our life together. To us, it meant, *You have my heart.*

A few seconds later, he was gone, and I stood there, bawling like a fool. But, for the first time since his death, I felt a sort of peace that had been missing.

Years have passed since then, and I am now an old woman. I still tend to the vegetable garden every day, and while I haven't seen William again, I feel his presence with me, even though he is no longer here. Our garden has become a place of comfort for me, a place where I can come to remember the love that we shared.

I know that the day will come when I will join William in the afterlife and that we will be reunited once again. But until then, I will continue to spend the warm days in the garden and know he's watching over me.

BACKWOODS ENCOUNTER

Witness: Larry McCarthy

Location: Fairfield County, Connecticut

. . .

My PARENTS SPLIT up when I was sixteen. It was a pretty acrimonious situation, and I hated being stuck in the middle of it. I asked if I could spend the summer with my gramps, and to my relief, they agreed.

I'd spent time with him before, about five days or a week each year. He was such an interesting guy. A WWII veteran, a master carpenter, a painter, musician. To this day, he is still the best man I've ever known. I'd also made a couple friends in the area, so it was shaping up to be a pretty awesome, laid-back summer.

One night, a little after the fourth of July, me and my friends Tom, Dale, and Jared decided to go ride. Gramps had an old Toyota that he let me drive. It wasn't much to look at, but it was a workhorse. We had no destination in mind, just driving aimlessly, killing time on a lazy summer evening.

The windows were rolled down, and the warm breeze carried the sweet scent of blooming wildflowers. We were laughing and chatting about our plans for the rest of the summer when we noticed something peculiar up ahead.

There, on the side of the road, stood a group of

eight figures, each of them barely visible in the dimming light. As we approached, we realized that they were human or human-like, but something about them seemed... off.

Their skin was ashen and stretched tight over their skulls, their eyes sunken deep into their faces. They stood in silence, watching us pass, but their stares were unwavering and made us all uneasy.

We continued down the road, all of us silent, until Tom spoke up. "Did you guys see that?" We all had seen it, and our unease was palpable.

"They're just some weirdos or something," I said, trying to shrug it off. But deep down, I sensed it was more than that. There was something off about those people, something that made my skin want to creep away.

As we drove further, we caught sight of them again, now emerging from the dense woods that surrounded us. There were more of them now, all of them standing still and staring at us with their sunken, dark eyes.

We began to panic, unsure of what was happening. Suddenly, one of them stepped forward, and we saw that it was holding something in its hand. It was a large knife, like a machete.

We all screamed, and I hit the gas pedal, the Toyota sputtering as it tried to gain speed. Those creepy people began to swarm us, their twisted faces illuminated in the headlights.

As we sped away, I could hear them pounding on the car, their breath coming in labored gasps. It was like something out of a nightmare, and I knew that we had to get out of there before it was too late.

They chased us through the winding, curving roads of the Connecticut woods. They were fast, much faster than we had anticipated, and I knew that we were in serious danger.

Finally, we spotted a clearing up ahead, and I swerved the car onto a dirt path, hoping that it would lead us to safety. The group was close behind, their screams echoing through the woods.

We crashed through the underbrush, the car lurching and bouncing over rocks and fallen branches. I could see that my friends were as terrified as I was. Dale wouldn't admit it now, but he was crying. I bet every one of us chucked our underwear in the trash when we got home.

Just as we thought we had lost them, more of the creeps burst from the treeline in front of us. I threw the car in reverse, doing a wild one eighty, when suddenly, there was a loud bang, and the car came to a screeching halt. We had hit an old fence post, and I could see that the trunk was smashed in.

"Get us out of here!" Jared screamed as the

creeps ran toward us.

I shifted back into first, stomped on the gas, and lurched forward. Fortunately, that reliable Toyota was still capable. We ripped through the clearing until we found an old driveway, then followed it to the main road.

I was focusing on driving and not crashing (again), but my friends told me they watched the creeps retreat back into the woods, disappearing in the trees. We were safe but shaken.

We eventually made our way back home, driving in silence and lost in our own thoughts. We didn't talk about what had happened until we got back to my gramps' house. He saw the car, and we pretty much had to tell him. Otherwise, he'd think I was drunk or something.

Well, after we told him what had gone down, he didn't call us crazy or accuse us of lying. He believed us without question. He told us that we had a run-in with the *melon heads* and went on to fill us in about the urban legend that had gone around that neck of the woods decades earlier.

I don't know if the group we saw really were melon heads or just some backwoods clan that got its laughs scaring dumb kids... like us... But to us, at that moment, they were real, and they were terrifying.

MY GRANDPARENTS' GHOST

Witness: Christina M.

Location: Essex, Vermont

. . .

THERE HAD ALWAYS BEEN whispers in our family about my grandparents' estate. Stories of hauntings and ghosts and unexplainable happenings. But I never truly believed them until I saw it for myself.

I was sixteen and visiting for a week over summer break. I won't lie, I'd have preferred to be going to the beach with my friends, but I also knew my grandparents were getting older, and I didn't want to miss a chance for more time with them.

The visit was going fine until my second night there. The estate was huge, with sprawling gardens and multiple buildings. Even though I come from a big family, none of my cousins or aunts and uncles were around. It was just grammy and popsy, their two workers, and me, but it always felt like someone was watching me.

That evening, I was in the main house exploring the upstairs study, fascinated by the leatherbound books, grand furniture, and antique decor. I'd just pulled down an early edition of *The Grapes of Wrath*, when I saw someone walk into the room. I turned to see who it was, but there was no one there. I shrugged it off and continued my exploration.

Later that night, as I was getting ready for bed, I

heard a sound coming from the hallway. It was footsteps, slow and deliberate, but when I checked the hall, it was empty. I closed the door and locked it, but I couldn't shake the feeling that I wasn't alone.

The following afternoon, I was in the gardens, admiring the astonishing variety of flowers, when I saw a figure in white up ahead. At first, I thought it was just someone coming to visit, or maybe a gardener.

As I moved toward them, I realized that it was a woman in a long white dress, the kind you see in old paintings. But what really got my attention was the fact that she was floating about four inches above the ground.

The ghost was turned away from me, and I couldn't see its face, so I began to circle around, making sure to keep plenty of distance. Just in case, you know? I wanted to see maybe it was someone I'd recognize from the dozens of old photographs framed throughout the house. But before I could get a look, a breeze kicked up, and the ghost seemed to break apart like smoke in the wind. Then, within seconds, it was gone entirely.

I was excited, but also a little unnerved. I wouldn't say I was scared, just unsettled, so I tried to pretend like it was no big deal. But then I started to hear whispers, voices that seemed to be coming from all around me. They were faint at first, but they grew louder as I walked deeper into the gardens. I couldn't make out what they were saying. It was just incomprehensible murmuring.

Nothing else occurred until the last day of my vacation. Popsy asked me to go to the carriage house and grab a ledger. The building, which had been preserved to look just as it did in the 1800s, had mostly just been used for storage for the last several decades.

As I climbed the stairs to where the documents were kept, I felt like I was being followed. I turned around several times, but no one was there. Then, when I was four steps away from the landing, I heard the melodic sound of a woman humming coming from above.

As I approached, the humming grew louder, and I could make out the tune. It was an old lullaby. *My Bonnie Lies Over the Ocean.* I pushed open the door and saw the ghost, the same one I'd seen in the garden, or at least the same dress. She was floating, looking out the window and into the night.

The sight, combined with the humming, made the whole situation feel dreamlike and weirdly peaceful. Well, for a moment anyway. She must have heard me enter the room and swiveled toward me.

I held my breath, expectant and eager to finally see her face. I thought she looked around twenty, with large eyes and a small cleft in her chin. But I only got a split second look at her pale, semi-transparent skin before she unleashed a blood-curdling scream. Her mouth opened wide, so wide it could fit a human head. Inside that gaping mouth was a black chasm. It looked bottomless.

I screamed in shock; I couldn't help myself. When I did that, she vanished into thin air as fast as someone turning off a light switch. I stumbled backward and tripped over a loose section of the rug. I fell into the wall, catching myself just before I could fall.

My heart pounding in my chest, I ran out of the building as fast as I could. While I ran, her scream kept echoing inside my head like a memory that refused to go away.

I didn't tell anyone about my experiences, and when Popsy asked about the ledger, I told him I couldn't find it. I spent the rest of the evening examining all of the photographs, but I hadn't gotten a good enough look at the ghost. If she was one of the women in the pictures, I sure couldn't place her.

I visited my grandparents a few more times before age caught up with them and they sold the estate, moving to Arizona. I didn't have any more ghost sightings there, or anywhere else for that matter, but I'm a believer.

LIGHTSHOW FROM ABOVE

WITNESS: TODD LANE

LOCATION: Canaan, Connecticut

· · ·

I'VE ALWAYS LOVED CAMPING. The feeling of being out in nature, disconnected from the hustle and bustle of the world, was something that I just found incredibly rejuvenating. So, when my friend Calvin suggested taking a weekend-long camping trip at a nearby lake, I didn't hesitate to accept.

Well, the morning we were supposed to leave finally arrived, and I woke up to a text from Calvin. He'd just come down with the stomach flu and wouldn't be able to go. I felt bad for him, but I was also frustrated with the situation. I'd really been looking forward to the trip. After stewing about it for a little while, I began to unload my Subaru. Then I thought, why not go anyway?

Sure, it wasn't the trip we'd been planning, but it would still be a weekend away, and really, that had been the main purpose. So, I threw everything back in the car and hit the road. I stopped at the grocery store since Calvin was going to bring the food, and I loaded up on munchies, protein bars, hot dogs, water, and (of course) some beer. After all, what's camping without tilting back a cold one?

I rolled into the lake around noon. After setting up my tent, I gathered together some firewood but didn't light it up right away. I just wanted to chill first. And, believe me, I did. By the time evening rolled around, I was feeling more relaxed, more like myself, than I had in months. This was exactly what I needed.

I started the fire as dusk set in, then cooked a few hot dogs over the coals. I swear, nothing tastes better than a hot dog cooked over an open flame. It's just the perfect combination of smokiness and saltiness. Better than anything I'd get in a five star restaurant, I'm sure.

Eventually, I got tired enough that I retreated to my tent. I didn't fall asleep right away, though. I just laid there, listening to the sound of the crickets and the gentle lapping of the water against the shore, a concert put on by Mother Nature.

I had my eyes shut, waiting to drift off, but through my closed eyelids, I suddenly saw a blinding bright burst of light. I thought it was lightning and groaned. Most of my gear was lying outside, and I didn't want to have to drag it all into the tent or throw it in the car. As I debated getting up, I realized something strange. There had been lightning but no thunder.

Heat lightning is nowhere near that bright, so my curiosity got the best of me. I unzipped the tent and poked my head outside. That was when I saw another light rise up from behind the trees in the near distance.

At first, I thought it might be a plane or a helicopter, but as I watched, it began to move in strange, jerky motions that no aircraft I knew of could replicate. I scrambled out of my tent and made my way toward the edge of the lake where my view wouldn't be quite as obscured by the trees.

Once there, I could see that the light was coming from a metallic, saucer-shaped object. And the object was moving... toward me. I was fascinated and terrified in equal measure. My heart was thudding in my chest as I stood there, motionless and in awe.

The craft drifted over me, toward the center of the lake. Once there, it stopped and just hovered. All the while, I didn't make a sound, no roaring of jets or the annoying *whop whop whop* of a chopper.

Suddenly, what had been a steady downward beam of light coming from the underside of the object began to pulse and flash in a rhythmic pattern. It was almost as if the light was some kind of code, flashing on and off in a way that was too deliberate to be random.

The air felt electric, like there was a current running through it. I could feel it all through my body, a tingling tension. I glanced down at the lakewater and saw it was shimmering, the way water does when it's on the verge of coming to a boil.

This went on for at least ten minutes. Then, the UFO began to move again, rising straight up without making a sound. Up and into the sky. As it flew, the lightshow it was emitting continued, and I could see the reflection of the light on the surface of the water below.

As the UFO disappeared from view, I was left standing there, alone on the shore of the lake, feeling both exhilarated and unnerved. What had I just seen? Was it really a UFO, or was there some other explanation for what I had witnessed?

I spent the rest of the night pacing back and forth, trying to make sense of what had happened. The lightshow was still imprinted on my mind, and I couldn't shake the feeling that there was some kind of message in it. But what could it be?

As the sun began to rise, I made my way back to my tent, exhausted but unable to sleep. I spent the rest of the day wandering around the lake, searching for some sort of hard evidence, like charred leaves, anything. But there was nothing to be found. I kept hoping I'd find other campers, someone who had seen what I'd seen. I traversed the entire eastern side of the lake, but there was no one to be found.

It was frustrating and isolating, and I wondered if I was going nuts. But the memory of that night stayed with me, haunting me with its unanswered questions. I didn't tell anyone what I'd seen for fear of their judgment, not even Calvin.

I kept hoping I'd forget all about it, so I could put it all behind me. But days turned into weeks, and weeks turned into months, and I still couldn't let go of what I had seen. I began to research UFO sightings and alien encounters, trying to find an explanation. But the more I read, the more confused I became.

I even resorted to putting a classified ad in a local newspaper, asking if anyone had seen a strange sight (without giving details) on the night of my encounter. But several more weeks passed with no response.

Then, one day, when I was on the verge of giving up, I received a letter in the mail. It was postmarked from a town a few hours away, and it was addressed to me by name. Inside, there was a single piece of paper with a message penned in tight, formal handwriting.

It read, "I saw the spaceship too."

I read it a thousand times, reassuring myself

that it was real. I couldn't believe I had finally found someone who could understand what I was going through. The letter didn't provide any more details, but just knowing that I wasn't alone eased the anxiety that had been almost overwhelming me.

I tried to track down the sender of the letter, but it was a dead end. I even went to the post office in the town in which it was postmarked. I asked the clerk if she recognized the writing. She didn't and looked at me like I was pretty crazy, but I didn't let that discourage me.

Instead, I began to reach out to other people who had reported UFO sightings in and around New England. Slowly but surely, I began to build a network of people who have seen strange lights in the sky, hovering objects, and other inexplicable phenomena.

Now, we meet up regularly, sharing stories and trying to piece together the puzzle of what we saw. To say this changed my life is a massive understatement. The camaraderie of my fellow witnesses was a balm to my soul, a reminder that I am not alone.

In the end, I never did get a definitive answer to the mystery of the UFO I had seen that night at the lake or its dazzling light show. But what I did find was a sense of community, a sense of wonder and possibility that had been missing from my life for far too long.

Now, when I look up at the night sky, I see it with new eyes. Eyes that are open to the possibility of something greater than ourselves, something that we may not yet fully understand.

DEMON IN MY HOUSE

WITNESS: ANONYMOUS

LOCATION: Central Falls, Rhode Island

. . .

I NEVER BELIEVED IN SPIRITS, monsters, or anything supernatural. I was always the one to roll my eyes when someone told me a supposedly true ghost story. Maybe that's why moving into my new home proved to be such a nightmare.

I'd been saving up for years before I could afford to move out of my crappy apartment. The house I ended up buying was small and old and needed a lot of work. It was a fixer-upper to say the least, but I saw the potential in it. I decided to take on the project of remodeling it myself. Well, with the help of *This Old House* reruns.

It wasn't long after I started the renovations that odd things began to happen. At first, everything was easily dismissible. Strange creaks and groans. Doors opening and closing on their own. Objects falling over. I brushed it off as the quirks of an old house. Something normal and harmless.

But then, the strange occurrences became more frequent and more inexplicable. One day, I walked into the kitchen to find that the cabinets had been opened, and several dishes were broken on the floor. I tried to tell myself it was shifting due to the house settling, but even I wasn't buying my own lies.

Another day, I was in the living room, painting the walls, when I heard footsteps coming from upstairs. I called out, thinking that maybe someone had broken in, but no one answered. I slowly walked up the stairs, my heart pounding in my chest, but there was no one there, and all of the windows were closed and locked from the inside.

Things only got worse from there. One night, as I was sleeping, I felt something tug at my leg. I opened my eyes to see a figure standing at the foot of my bed. It was a dark black shadow. I opened my mouth to scream, but no sound came out.

The figure moved closer to me, and the room turned so cold that I could see my own breath. I squeezed my eyes shut, praying this was a bad dream. When I opened them again, it was gone, but it took hours for the room to get back to normal temperature.

I spent the next few days in a state of constant fear. I could feel its presence everywhere I went in the house. The air was heavy and oppressive, and I could hardly sleep at night because I was afraid it would show up again, and the next time, maybe it wouldn't go away.

The following week, an electrician came to the house to upgrade some old wiring. He was working in the basement, and I was putting flooring down in the bedroom when I heard him yell out in pain. I ran down to find him lying on the ground, moaning and his body shaking. When he recovered, he told me he'd just received the worst shock of his life. We both went to the electrical panel, and all of the breakers for the basement were switched on. He was absolutely certain he'd turned them off before beginning his work.

The very next day, I walked into the living room, and I saw something that still makes me feel sick just thinking about it. A viscous black fluid was running down the freshly painted walls, pooling on the floor. It looked almost like tar but had a strong sulfur-like smell. I couldn't believe what I was seeing and burst into tears.

I could no longer write this off as some harmless ghost. I knew then that I couldn't keep living in the house, not like this. I needed help, and the only person I could think of was a priest.

I reached out to the local church, and they put me in touch with a kind, older gentleman who'd been with the church for decades. I went there to meet with him and tell him everything that had happened. I expected him to start laughing, but he listened very patiently and took me seriously. When I finished, he said he wanted to help me and that he wanted to see my house as soon as possible because he believed it was infested with a demon.

I was terrified, and we went straight to the house. I walked with him as he went from room to room, reciting scripture and sprinkling holy water. After he blessed every room, we returned to the living room. I'd cleaned up the black goo, but you could still see faint, rusty stains on the white walls and laminate floor.

We knelt and held hands and prayed together for at least half an hour. The longer it went, the more I realized that some of that heaviness and dread I'd been feeling was fading. When we finished, I took a deep breath, opened my eyes, and felt more free and hopeful than I had in weeks.

But just a few days later, I was painting in the kitchen when I heard a loud noise outside. I got up to investigate and saw that a flock of starlings had slammed into the house, shattering two windows and killing many of the birds. Dozens more laid on the ground, twitching and dazed.

I worried that the demon was still there, that it was fighting back. I immediately went back to the church and told the priest what had happened. He returned to the house, blessing it again and ordering the demon out. We prayed until the sun set. It must have been hours.

After the second blessing, there was no further activity. In the coming months, I finished all of my remodeling projects. It was finally *my* home in every way.

I still live there, almost twenty years later, only now it's with my teenage son. We've made countless wonderful memories within these walls. I've shared my story with a few friends over the years, and they always ask me why I didn't move and if I feel safe here. I understand their concern, but I wholly believe that our happiness, coupled with the power of God, has vanquished the demon forever.

VISIT FROM BEYOND

WITNESS: JUSTIN

LOCATION: Bangor, Maine

. . .

I was eleven when my next-door neighbor, Harry, died. He was an older guy, a retired lobsterman, and as crotchety as they come. I don't remember a lot about him, but what sticks in my mind was him always grumbling about one thing or another. Our grass was too long, our trees were dropping leaves in his yard, etc.

Harry was a widower. I never knew his wife. She'd died before I was even born. He had two grown sons who'd both moved away. So, it was just him rambling around in his little house. I'd imagine it got lonely and boring.

Almost every time my friends and I rode our bikes past Harry's house, he'd come busting out the door, shaking his fist and hollering at us about being on the sidewalk. He was never scary, though, and it was just part of the neighborhood routine. Looking back, I think it just gave him something to do. He'd always holler, "You kids should be riding on the street!" To Harry, everyone under the age of fifty was just called Kid. He even called my dad, Kid.

Anyway, he died—I think of a heart attack—and my parents took me to the viewing to pay our respects. I'd never been to a funeral home before, and I'd definitely never seen a for real dead person.

I wasn't sure how to feel leading up to it. I didn't know Harry well enough to feel sad. I probably wasn't even old enough to really comprehend death. And, I guess this might sound strange, but there was a morbid fascination about the whole process. Getting dressed up in nice clothes, the kind we wore to church, walking up to the funeral home which had a doorman who pointed us toward the correct room, writing your name in a random book. It was all so new and... weird.

When we got to the room where Harry was laid out, I immediately noticed the pitch black casket up front. It had its own lights shining down on it, and it was surrounded by ornate flower arrangements. It seemed like a shrine. Again, weird.

Lots of people were there, some of them crying, some laughing and sharing stories and memories. The line we had to wait in to get to Harry's family was long and winding. But, about five minutes into it, my bladder started screaming. I kept wriggling and swaying, trying to stave off the need to go, but it was a useless battle.

I eventually gave up and tugged on my dad's jacket sleeve, telling him I needed to use the bathroom. He pointed me toward a hallway and left me to wander off on my own. I found it, though, just in time. After washing my hands and coming back out, I almost ran into a middle-aged woman. She was just standing there outside the bathroom, and I assumed she had to go too.

I apologized for almost bumping into her, and she waved her hand to signify it was no big deal. I stepped around her, heading back to my parents, but for some reason, I stopped and glanced back. She was still standing there, all alone. She hadn't gone into the bathroom, which I found bizarre because why stand there otherwise? So, I asked, "Ma'am, are you okay?"

She took a long look at me, and a small smile tugged at her lips. She nodded, then said in a breathy, faint voice, "Harry says, 'Thanks for coming, kid.'"

I found that a strange thing to say, speaking for a dead guy. But sometimes, adults like to mess with kids, so I didn't think too much about it.

When I got back to the viewing room, my parents were near the front of the line, with just two couples ahead of them. I rejoined them, not saying anything about the woman outside the bathroom. By the time we reached Harry's sons, I'd almost forgotten about her altogether.

I had to stand on my tiptoes to look into Harry's casket. I don't know what I had been expecting, but it wasn't that. He looked like Harry, but at the same time, not. I could tell they had put makeup on him, which seemed all kinds of wrong. His cheeks were rosy, but the rest of him was pale and almost gray.

While my parents talked to Harry's sons, I busied myself by looking at the flowers and reading the cards that came with them. There was a folded U.S. flag, and beside it a framed picture of a young man in an Army uniform. I'd never known Harry was a vet until then.

There were other photos too, a whole board of them. Most were small prints held on with thumbtacks, but in the center was a formal portrait, the kind my family had taken in church every other year. I think even the background was the same as one of ours.

In that portrait was Harry, his age somewhere in between that of the soldier version and the old man I knew. He was recognizable, though, just more hair—and darker hair—than I was used to seeing. But what made me gasp was the woman in the picture with him. She was the woman I'd seen standing outside the bathroom. The one who had spoken to me.

As I was staring at her, one of Harry's sons leaned over my shoulder and said, "That was my mom. I don't think you ever met her."

My mouth was too dry to speak, so I just shook my head. He patted me on the shoulder and thanked me for being a good neighbor to his dad, and with that, we were moving on.

Before we left, I told my dad I needed to use the bathroom again. He raised an eyebrow and asked if I had drunk too much milk at supper or something, and I said I guess so and hurried back to the bathroom.

The hallway was empty. I checked the bathroom, and it was empty too. The woman—Harry's long-dead wife—was nowhere to be found.

REFLECTIONS IN FEAR

WITNESS: JANE W.

. . .

LOCATION: Kent, Connecticut

I'M NOT GOING to lie; I can't pass up a good tag sale. The allure of finding a valuable antique, some hidden treasure, is impossible to resist. Before the internet took off, I'd prowl the newspaper ads, cruise the back roads, anything necessary to find a good deal. I suppose it's an addiction, albeit a harmless one. Well, at least it started off that way...

The ad claimed *Antiques, Collectibles, Vintage Clothing & Much More!* How could I not check it out? The sellers lived in an old Victorian house. As I checked out their wares, I struck up a conversation with them. They'd just purchased the house and were planning to remodel and resell it. What people these days call *flipping*. They bought it with all of the contents included but weren't keeping any of it. They wanted a clean slate, they said.

Their loss was my gain, though, as I stumbled upon a beautiful, framed mirror that I knew I had to have. It had the most lovely wood frame, with delicate carvings, the kind that can only be made by hand. The glass itself had a wonderful patina too. I checked the price tag and was shocked to see it fit within my budget. After handing over the cash, it was mine. They even wrapped it up in bubble wrap and helped me put it in my car.

I had the perfect spot for it in my living room. As soon as I got home, I eagerly unpacked the mirror and hung it on the wall, admiring the way it caught the light and how perfectly it fit in with the rest of my decor

My excitement was short-lived, though, because later that day, I started to notice odd happenings. At first, it was just little things; a flicker of movement in the corner of my eye, a whisper that I couldn't quite make out. But soon, things escalated.

I started seeing reflections in the mirror, reflections of things that couldn't possibly be there. Shadows that moved on their own, figures that darted across the glass too quickly to make out. And then there were the voices that seemed to emanate from the mirror itself. Soft at first, like whispers on the wind, but growing louder and more insistent with each passing day.

I tried to ignore it, chalking it up to my imagination or the stress of my job, which hadn't been going well of late. But as the days wore on, things only got worse. I started seeing ghosts in the mirror. Apparitions that seemed to come from another time and place. Men in vintage suits. Women in expensive Victorian-era gowns. And children. So many children.

But what was especially unnerving about the images was that all the people I was seeing were clearly dead. Their eyes were dull and lifeless. Their faces rigid and unmoving. Their flesh pallid and gray. I'd always believed in ghosts but had never seen any or had any unusual experiences of my own. It was oddly exciting and only slightly disturbing. Nothing I couldn't handle.

And then, one night, I witnessed something that still gives me nightmares. I was sitting on the couch when I saw myself in the mirror. But it wasn't really me. It was an up-close image of me, like I was standing right in front of it.

The reflection showed me with wild eyes and a twisted grin, holding a butcher's knife to my own throat. As I watched, the reflected version of me plunged the knife into my neck, twisting the blade to maximize the carnage. Blood gushed out, saturating my clothes. I watched myself die in that mirror and couldn't hold back a scream that was loud enough to elicit a call from my neighbor to make sure everything was okay.

I tried to hide away the mirror, but it seemed to

cling to me like a curse. I put it in the attic, and the next morning, it was back on the wall of the living room. I shoved it in a storage shed in the backyard, but later that day, it was lying on my kitchen table. I put it on the curb along with a sign reading free, but days went by, and no one claimed it, and on the third day, it was back on the wall, even though I hadn't put it there.

Finally, in a fit of desperation, I laid the mirror on the driveway, then grabbed a shovel from the garage. I must have looked like a madwoman to anyone watching, but I didn't care. I stood over the mirror, swinging the shovel again and again. I shattered the glass, splintered the frame. I didn't stop until it was a pile of rubble. Then I used the shovel for its intended purpose, scooped up all of the pieces, and dumped them in the trash can.

It felt like an elephant had been lifted off of my shoulders, but when I went to bed, I got the idea that somehow, the mirror would piece itself back together, like that car in *Christine*. I was sure that when I awoke in the morning, it would be back in the living room, and my reflection would be laughing at me, laughing until it drove me mad.

Fortunately, my fears were for naught. When I woke in the morning, I checked every inch of the house, and the mirror was nowhere to be found.

The trash had been collected earlier that morning, and when I checked the can, it, too, was empty. Finally, I was rid of the cursed thing.

I still go to tag sales—I just can't help myself—but no more mirrors for me.

GHOST RIDER

Witness: Jim Grant

Location: Worcester, Massachusetts

. . .

I'VE ALWAYS BEEN a creature of habit. Every morning, I catch the 6:30 a.m. bus to work. I sit in the same seat, pull out the current book I'm reading, and lose myself in the pages until we reach my stop. For years, this routine went on without interruption, but that changed back in 2013.

One Wednesday morning, I was sitting in my usual spot, reading my book, when I noticed a woman take the seat across from me. She was dressed in an old-fashioned outfit, sort of hippie clothes, like you would have seen at Woodstock. She wore a long floral print dress and a sun bonnet on her head. I didn't think much of it. Maybe she was going to a costume party or was some sort of performer.

She didn't make eye contact or speak to me, nor any of the other riders. She didn't read a book or page through a magazine or waste time on her phone. She just stared straight, never even glancing at the other riders as they came and went. She was still on the bus when I came to my stop about twenty minutes later.

I'd pretty much forgotten about her until the next day when she showed up again. She took the same seat and was wearing the same clothes. The next day, the scene repeated itself. Over the weekend, I realized she was in my thoughts almost constantly. Who was this odd woman?

On Monday, I could barely pay attention to my book. I just kept waiting for her to show up, but enough time passed that I assumed she wasn't going to return. I started reading, and then, the next time I looked up, she was in her usual seat, wearing the same flower child clothing. But what was even more strange was that there hadn't been any stops since I'd last checked her seat.

Had she been on the bus all along? Maybe sitting up front, and then moved to the back where she usually sat? I was beyond curious but kept my questions to myself.

Every day that week, she arrived on the bus after me, still wearing the same clothes, still not interacting with anyone. I started to wonder if maybe she was homeless or had some kind of mental illness.

But then I started to notice other things that made me think she was something more than just a random homeless person. For one thing, nobody else ever seemed to acknowledge her presence. People would get on and off the bus, squeezing past her or sitting next to her, without so much as a glance in her direction. It was as if they didn't see her at all.

I tried to shake it off and convince myself that I was just being paranoid. But then, one morning, as I was getting off the bus, I heard a voice whisper in my ear. It was faint and ghostly, but I could make out the words, "I know you watch me."

I spun around, but nobody was there. The woman in the bonnet was still sitting in her usual spot, staring straight ahead. Silent and emotionless.

That's when I decided to talk to the bus driver. I approached him one morning as I boarded and asked him about the hippy woman in the bonnet. At first, he looked at me like I was insane. But when I described her in detail, down to the color of her eyes, he went white as a sheet.

"What are you trying to pull?" he asked.

I said that I wasn't trying to pull anything, that I was just being curious. He glared at me for a moment, then muttered, "One of the old drivers hit a woman who was dressed just like you said. Hit and killed her on this route. But that was over fifty years ago."

I felt light-headed and on the verge of passing out. It seemed impossible. But the more I thought about it, the more it made sense. Nobody ever acknowledged her because she wasn't really there.

And that whisper in my ear? It had to be her, trying to reach out from the other side.

As strange as it sounds, I started to look forward to my morning commutes. I felt like I had a connection with this woman who had died so many years ago, and it was a connection that nobody else could understand.

I tried to make contact with her, talking to her, moving into the seat beside her, but she never reacted in any way. The other riders must have thought I'd lost it and began avoiding me, so I eventually stopped trying to talk to her.

I rode that bus for four more years until I was promoted and transferred to our office in Boston. And for all of those years, she was there every day, riding the bus to a destination that I suppose she never reached.

Sometimes, I think about taking a day off work, driving to my old hometown, catching my old bus, and seeing if she's still around. I'd wager that she is. After all, she seemed to enjoy the ride.

TRESPASSING IN CORNWALL

PRIOR TO THE INTERVIEW:

"Is it okay if I don't use my real name? I want to talk about what happened, but this isn't one of my proudest moments."

Interviewer: "Of course."

Cool. Then call me Randy. I always thought that would be a funny name."

Interviewer: "As you wish."

WITNESS: "RANDY"

Location: Cornwall, Connecticut

I SWEAR, every teenager in Western Connecticut has heard the stories about Dudleytown. The prevailing legend—at least, the way I heard it—was that the original owners (the Dudleys) had been chased out of England for trying to overthrow the King. But banishment wasn't punishment enough. First, the patriarch of the family was beheaded, and then a curse was placed on all of his ancestors, a curse that followed them to the new world as they settled in Connecticut in the mid 1700s.

The family had intended to become farmers, but the plot of land they bought was mountainous and heavily shaded, oftentimes leaving the land in virtual darkness, even at high noon. To this day, that area is still known as the "Dark Entry Forest."

When the Dudleys realized farming wasn't going to work out, they turned to mining iron ore, which was somewhat more successful as the ground was rocky and rugged. They used many of those rocks to build their houses and outbuildings.

Dudleytown eventually grew to host more than twenty families, but prosperity and happiness proved elusive. Sickness was common, odd accidental deaths happened frequently, and many people, especially children, vanished never to be seen again. Insanity and madness also ran rampant.

Over the decades, the population dwindled, and the whole town ended up as a parcel of land purchased by a wealthy New York doctor seeking a quiet weekend retreat in the country. It's said that he had returned to the city for business, leaving his wife alone on the property. Upon his return, he found she'd lost her mind and was ranting about strange creatures emerging from the woods at night and attacking her. She took her own life soon thereafter.

The buildings on the property eventually decayed and crumbled, and all that remains today are hollowed-out basements and the stone foundations. While that might not sound too exciting, for a goth kid in the 90s, it was more intriguing than Disneyland, and I had to see it in person. I just needed a set of wheels.

After I turned sixteen, I *inherited* a piece of

crap '79 Chevy Caprice station wagon. It had been my mom's, then my older sister's, and then mine. I wasn't going to complain, though. Wheels are wheels, after all, and it hadn't cost me a dime.

A few months later, in the summer before my junior year, I figured I had enough experience on the road to drive out to Dudleytown and visit the place I'd heard and read so much about. I left in the early afternoon and rolled in around three. There's no actual road into the ruins, so I parked and decided to walk the rest of the way. But not before grabbing the spirit board out of my trunk. Yeah, I know... Like I said earlier, not one of my proudest moments.

The hike didn't take too awfully long, but the terrain was pretty rugged. I grabbed a dead tree branch to use as a walking stick, while keeping the spirit board tucked under my other arm, and the planchette in my pocket. Going was slow, to say the least.

I eventually made it to where some of the buildings stood, and it was only then that I realized how dark it was. I checked my watch and saw it still wasn't even four o'clock, but I was down in the valley, and the trees were crazy tall and thick, so it made sense. What didn't make as much sense, though, was how quiet it all was. I spent a fair amount of time in the woods, and you always hear signs of life. Bugs buzzing by your ears. Squirrels hopping across dead leaves. Birds serenading from above. But down there, in Dudleytown, it was dead quiet. The only sounds I heard were the ones I made.

After exploring the ruins, I decided to take a seat on one of the larger foundations. Then, I set the spirit board on my lap, took out the planchette, and decided to get the show on the road.

"Is anyone here with me?" I asked.

I waited a few seconds, then a minute. No movement from the planchette. So, I tried again.

"Will a resident of Dudleytown please communicate with me?" I asked.

A few more seconds passed. Long enough that I was convinced nothing would happen. Then, suddenly, the planchette jerked to the Yes marker so fast that it almost flew out of my hands.

I was creeped out but also wildly excited. After all, that was why I was there.

"Were you one of the Dudley's?" I asked.

The board answered, "No."

"Then who were you?"

Slowly, the planchette spelled out "D-C-T-O-R W-I.F."

I was practically bouncing with excitement.

"What did you see in the forest? What drove you crazy?" I asked.

No answer.

"What attacked you?" I tried.

After another, even longer pause, I got an answer. "D-E-M-N-S."

"Demons?" I asked.

The planchette snapped to YES, and then something slapped the board out of my hands. It somersaulted through the air and landed in the basement of one of the old foundations.

I stood up, about to climb down to and retrieve it when I felt... not hands, but a... some kind of force, slam into my back. It was hard enough to knock me off balance, and no matter how much I waved my arms, trying to regain it, I was too far gone.

I fell about eight feet into the hole of the foundation, landing on my side in a puddle of stagnant water. As I scrambled to my feet, I saw what I can only describe as a black cloud, like a cloud of smoke, floating above me. But it didn't move like smoke. It had a... purpose, I guess I'd say. It floated across the foundation, to the opposite side, then stopped. Like it was looking down on me.

I left the spirit board behind, grabbed the stone walls, and dragged myself out of the basement.

When I had made it out, I looked back and saw the black cloud rocketing toward me.

I turned and ran as fast as I could go. I don't know how many times I fell, tripping over rocks and branches and my own two feet. I sliced my forearm open on a piece of a broken bottle, carving a nice four-inch gash that left a scar that remains to this day. But every time I fell, I bounced back up and ran even faster.

I had made it about halfway up the hillside when I risked looking back. I immediately wished I hadn't. That smoke, or cloud, or whatever it was, was right on my heels, and looking back had caused me to slow down enough for it to reach me.

It didn't grab me or knock me down, though. Instead, it just sort of washed over me. It felt like a blast of winter air hitting me at forty-miles-per-hour, but even worse was how it made me feel. All of a sudden, I was overwhelmed with an almost crippling sense of dread. I just felt completely hopeless. If there had been a bridge nearby, I have no doubt I would have jumped off of it.

I dropped to my knees, sobbing uncontrollably. And then I guess I passed out.

When I woke up, it was dark, and not because I was in the forest. My watch was broken, but I could see the moon poking through trees above.

As shocking as it was to realize I'd just lost hours, I was still relieved because that feeling of sadness and despair was gone. I felt like myself again. I stood up, brushed myself off, and trudged back through the woods and to my car.

When I got there, I saw a state police cruiser parked behind my station wagon. The trooper was inside his car, waiting for me. He stepped out as I approached, and once he got a good look at me, a little smirk pulled at his lips. My arm has stopped bleeding, but I was covered in dried blood, dirt, leaves, the works. I was a mess.

"Made it to Dudleytown, I see," the trooper said.

I was too tired, both physically and emotionally, to even try to come up with a lie. "Yes, sir," I said.

He nodded, knowing.

"How long have you been waiting for me?" I asked.

"Hour. Maybe an hour and a half."

"Why didn't you come and get me?" I asked.

He looked past me, toward the woods, and that little smirk faded away. He pulled out his ticket book and began writing my fine without answering. When he handed it over, he simply said, "It's private property, that's why. Of course, I trust you won't be making a return trip."

Without waiting for me to answer, he returned to his cruiser and drove off.

He was right, though. I never did go back. And I wouldn't recommend you visit Dudleytown either. If you do, you might not be as lucky as me and get away with only a fine.

NIGHT SCREAMS

WITNESS: TIM BLAKE

LOCATION: Wallagrass, Maine (approx.)

.   .   .

JASON, Paul, and I had been planning the fishing trip for months. One week (well, five days, but close enough) at a little lake so far north in Aroostook County that we might need to learn how to speak French. I'm originally from Bangor and had only been there once before, on a trip with my pop and uncles, way back when I was ten. I had good memories and couldn't wait to return.

I'd known Jason since his parents moved next door to mine when we were both in grade school. Paul came along later, in junior high, but once we connected, we were as thick as thieves, as the saying goes. Life had begun to pull us in different directions, though. Jason landed himself a cushy job with a software company and moved to Boston. Paul got married and was preparing to start a family in Veazie.

As for me, I still lived just a few miles from the house I grew up in. I had a job at the mill and tried to pretend like I wasn't an adult, even though all the signs kept telling me I was and that it was time to grow up and start acting like one.

But I wanted to put that off, and what better way to do that than with a fishing trip, right?

Truth be told, none of us were expert anglers.

We were just three guys in our early twenties who were excited about time away from work and our regular lives. Days on the boat, evenings by the campfire, nights in our tents. Fresh cooked fish and plenty of beers. Sounds damned near perfect, right?

We set off early on a crisp autumn morning, packed into Paul's pickup truck with all of our gear. None of us owned a boat, but I'd planned ahead and borrowed a big old canoe from a guy I worked with. He even threw in some life vests. We tied it to the roof of the pickup and prayed it wouldn't fall off on the drive.

Thankfully, it didn't, and we rolled up on the lake about four hours later. It was a beautiful spot, surrounded by dense forests and rolling hills. We set up our tents on the edge of the lake and wasted no time before hitting the water.

Several hours and some windburn later, all we had to show for our efforts was one brook trout that Paul caught. I scored a couple of creek chubs that went right back into the lake. Jason laid a goose egg. Not much of a haul, but none of us cared. We were together and having a blast.

That first night, we sat around the fire, talking, drinking, and laughing late into the night. The next two days and nights brought more of the same, with a few more fish and fuller bellies. On the fourth night, though, just as we were getting ready to turn in, we heard a bizarre, piercing noise emanate from deep inside the forest. It was a long, low wail, like a cry of pain or anguish. I bet it lasted around thirty seconds, and whatever had made it never needed to pause to take a breath.

We'd all spent our fair share of time in the woods growing up and knew what animals sounded like. I was sure I'd never heard anything like it, and from the looks on my friends' faces, neither had they.

"What the hell was that?" Jason asked, his eyes bulging and as wide as hard-boiled eggs.

My heart was thudding in my ears, and I couldn't get any words out. But Paul said, "An owl maybe?"

I knew it wasn't an owl, but I told myself maybe he was right. I wanted to believe it, anyway. We waited around, not talking anymore, just listening. But it didn't come again. We all turned in early that night, but not before stoking up the fire real good and throwing on enough wood to ensure it would blaze all night long.

By the time morning rolled around, the uneasy feeling left in the wake of that sound had faded to a dull memory, made even more hazy by a slight hangover. I'd pretty much convinced myself that I'd blown it out of proportion, and that Paul had been right after all. It was just an owl. None of us mentioned it at breakfast or throughout the day. It was like it never happened.

That day, we had our best day of fishing. I reeled in four trouts, and so did Jason. Paul only nabbed two but one was damned near a prize winner. At least, as far as fishing stories go. We couldn't eat them all that night and threw the rest in the cooler in case the next day was a bust.

I think we'd all pretty much forgotten about that creepy sound. Until we heard it again.

It happened after we were all in our tents, around one, maybe one-thirty in the morning. I'd been sawing logs, but it was so damned loud that I woke up straight off and sat up so fast I smashed my head against the roof of the tent. About that time, I heard a zipper being unzipped, and Paul asked, "You guys awake?"

I hurried out of the tent, swiping at my eyes to clear them of sleep. It was almost a full moon, so even though the campfire had burned down to embers, it wasn't hard to see. Paul was standing at the edge of our campsite, arms crossed over his chest and swaying a little from side to side as he stared into the woods. About that time, Jason popped out of his tent, pulling on a sweatshirt as he stumbled out. "That's no damn owl," Jason said to me.

He was right, of course. Even though owls can sound pretty creepy, especially late at night, this sound was coming from something larger than a bird. You could almost feel the power of it in its scream.

I yanked on my boots and jogged to Paul. "Did you see something?" I asked him.

He didn't answer for a long time. Didn't respond at all. So, I reached out and put my hand on his shoulder. At my touch, he jumped about a foot straight into the air. When he came down, he turned back to me, his face the color of ash. "Didn't see nothing," he said.

When you've been friends with someone for a long time, you can tell pretty easily when they're lying. And Paul was lying to me. But something about the look on his face, the fear in his eyes, made me not want to press him. Maybe because I was afraid of what he'd say if I did.

Jason arrived at our sides a few seconds later, and the three of us stood there in silence, just staring. And waiting. I don't know how much time passed—it felt like forever—but eventually, the sound came again. That screechy, mournful wail. It seeped through the trees and surrounded us.

Jason was the first to abandon ship. He didn't say a word either, just turned on his heels and booked it back to the tents. I threw a glance his way and noticed he was almost running. Now, Jason's a big guy. Six, three, about two and a half bills. Seeing him running, fleeing, made me want to do the same.

"Let's head back," I said to Paul. But he didn't react at all. He just stood there, like he was frozen in place. I grabbed his forearm and gave it a shake and that seemed to snap him out of whatever daze he was in. He gave a little nod and said, "Yeah, sure," and then we retreated to the camp.

When we got there, Jason was in his tent, but the flap was down, and I could see him sitting by the door. Moonlight reflected off something in his hands, and when I took a look, I realized he was holding a pistol.

We were all hunters and had been around guns all our lives, but that was the first time I ever saw another man holding a gun with the purpose of self-defense. And, let me tell you, it's entirely different from the way someone holds a gun when they're out scouting for deer or plunking cans off fence posts. Instead of making me feel safer or reassured, it made me even more nervous.

"I'll take first watch," Jason said.

Taking watch hadn't even occurred to me until that very moment, but once the words were out there, it seemed to make sense. Paul and I went into our tents. I don't know about him, but I know I didn't get a wink of sleep and was still wide awake when Jason checked on me a couple of hours later.

I took the second watch. Even though that sound hadn't resumed, I was as on edge as I'd ever been in my whole life. I spent most of the time stoking up the fire or checking and rechecking the pistol to make sure the ammunition hadn't magically disappeared. Every snapping branch or whistle of the wind almost made me soil my jeans, but I made it through.

When dawn broke, we all huddled around the fire, waiting for the coffee to heat up. None of us had anything to say. All of the good cheer and small talk had dried up. Or maybe it had been chased away by whatever had made those God-awful sounds.

Since the trip had been mostly my idea, I decided that getting it back on track was my burden to bear. I grabbed my tackle box and began rummaging through it, deciding on what bait to use to start the day. But I didn't even get a chance before Paul said, "I'm not going out on the water today." He wasn't looking at me when he said it. His eyes were on the woods.

I glanced at Jason, hoping he'd be on my side, but he wouldn't make eye contact. So, I said to Paul, "You're gonna waste the day sitting by the fire?"

Again, without looking at me, he said, "No. I'm going into the woods."

His tone left no room to negotiate. His mind was made up, and there was no changing it. Rather than try, I agreed to go with him. Jason did too. I grabbed a deer rifle that I keep in my truck, and without any further discussion, we pushed into the forest, moving in the direction those sounds had come from.

It was dark in those woods. The day was overcast in general, so that didn't help, but it seemed unnaturally dark. It might as well have been dusk instead of mid-morning, and the further we went, the more the light seemed to fade away. To die off.

I found myself wishing I'd have brought a flashlight. Not that I believe now that it would have helped. Because it didn't seem like the light was simply being blocked from the canopy of leaves above us. It was like something—some *thing*—was devouring it.

I guess that sounds crazy to you. It sounds crazy to me, and I was there. But that's how it felt.

Paul was in the lead with Jason, and I was a couple yards back. We hadn't seen anything out of the ordinary, and I was starting to believe we wouldn't. Then, ahead of us, Paul raised his right arm and made a halting motion.

I froze. I think one foot was still in mid air, like someone had hit the pause button. Paul said, or rather whispered, "Watch your step." He stayed put as Jason and I caught up to him. When we reached him, his warning made more sense. The ground was riddled with holes, and when I took a better look, I realized we were actually standing on enormous boulders, which were covered by a thin layer of decaying leaves, dirt, and forest debris. In between the boulders were plunging crevasses. Most weren't wide enough to fall into, but a wrong step could easily lead to a broken ankle or leg.

We kept moving forward, albeit at a snail's pace. It seemed foolish to me, and I suppose to Jason too because he said, "Let's go back before one of us gets hurt." I nodded in agreement, but before I could get my words out, Paul said, quite curtly, "Go if you want."

Maybe it's because we were still fairly young men and didn't want to look like chickens in front of our friend, or maybe we didn't want to leave Paul alone, but Jason and I continued to follow Paul across that stony land.

All of a sudden, we heard that wailing sound again. And it was close, so close it made my ears hurt. Like standing directly in front of a fire siren. I dropped my rifle as I tried to cover my ears, and the shrieking was so loud I didn't even hear it clatter against the stone.

When it finally stopped, Paul, who was still in the lead, darted forward in the direction from which the scream had come. That man was on a mission, one I wasn't sure I wanted to accept. But Jason followed after, and so did I.

We couldn't have crossed even ten yards when Paul skidded to a stop, so fast I saw his feet kick up the ground in a little whirlwind of disturbance. Jason reached his side and stopped too.

Feeling like I had no other choice, I joined them at the edge of one of those deep chasms, but this one was wider, probably three feet across. Plenty big enough for a man to fall into. And that's exactly what had happened.

But what was down in the crevasse was no man. At first, I thought it was a deer—a buck—because I saw its antlers, bone white, standing out in contrast against the darkness of the abyss. But then it looked up.

It had the head of a deer, but its skull was vacant of fur. It was skeletal aside from a few rotting clumps of tissue. It tilted its head back, like it was taking a good look at us, even though the eye sockets were empty, black holes. Then its jaw opened, and it unleashed a shriek, the same sound we'd heard so many times on that trip.

Before I could even cover my ears again to try to block out that painful screeching, Paul grabbed Jason's pistol and aimed it down at that... thing. He fired off two shots. Then two more. Rapid fire. The creature stopped screaming, but Paul wasn't finished. He shot again and again, until the magazine was empty. Then he pulled the trigger a few more times for good measure, resulting in empty clicks.

Down in that chasm, I saw the creature flee from the gunfire. It was an awkward, shambling gait. Like a newborn colt still getting the hang of walking. As it moved away from us, I saw it had the body of a man—or something man-like, anyway. It looked too long, too thin. Every bone was visible beneath its tautly stretched skin, like it had no muscle. Only flesh and bone with nothing in between.

It followed the path of the chasm, making clacking, hoof-like sounds against the rocks as it moved. And then it was far enough away in that deep, dark hole that I couldn't see it at all anymore.

Only then did I realize Paul was shaking. Tears streamed down his face. I took hold of the pistol and peeled it free of his sweaty grip, then passed it over to Jason. "Paul," I said. He didn't react. "Paul?"

He slowly came out of his trance, or his shock, or whatever he was experiencing. He looked to his hand and seemed surprised the gun wasn't there any more. "We have to go," I said. He didn't respond verbally, but when I began to turn him away from the crevasse and back toward our camp, he seemed to get the gist of it.

We were careful where we stepped but wasted no time as we returned to our campsite. Even though we had a couple of days left in our trip, without a word of discussion, we started packing up and didn't stop until the truck was loaded. We tossed out the uneaten fish for the wildlife to scavenge and snuffed out the fire.

As Paul and I were tying the canoe to the truck, I risked speaking up for the first time since we'd gotten back to camp. "What was that thing?" I asked.

He didn't answer for a long while, waiting until the last ropes were knotted off. Then, in barely above a whisper, he said one word. "Wendigo."

I think everyone from Maine has at least passing knowledge of the Wendigo. It's a Native American creature or evil spirit. Some people say it's a man who was transformed into that monstrosity as a curse. Other theories are that the spirit possesses men and turns them into blood-thirsty, flesh-eating cannibals.

As for the latter, I certainly didn't have an appetite after seeing it. I don't know if what we saw was actually a Wendigo or not, but after we got home, I looked up some paintings and drawings of them online, and the resemblance was uncanny. It gave me nightmares for weeks. Sometimes, I still dream of it.

Every now and again, I think about going back up to the lake and waiting. Listening. But over two decades have passed, and I haven't worked up the nerve.

Paul, Jason, and I never once spoke of the experience again. Truth be told, we didn't talk much at all after that. I haven't seen Jason in over ten years. Last I heard, he'd moved to Phoenix,

Arizona, which is about as far as you can get from the woods of Maine. Once in a while, I spot Paul at the county fair or the grocery store. We nod at each other and try to smile, but when I do see him, I see the same haunted look in his eyes that I see in my own every time I look in the mirror.

In a way, it's like we brought part of that thing back with us. And it will be with us forever.

AFTERWORD

I hope you've enjoyed New England's Unexplained Mysteries! If you've had any experiences you would like to share, please visit me on the web at www.TonyUrbanAuthor.com

Additionally, if you enjoyed this book then I know you will LOVE "Pennsylvania's Unexplained Mysteries," "Pennsylvania's Most Haunted Places,"and "Beware of the Woods."

Thank you so much for being a reader and for enjoying all sorts of unexplainable weirdness, just like me.

Until next time, stay scared!

Tony Urban

Also by Tony Urban
  Within the Woods
  Hell on Earth
  Her Deadly Homecoming

Made in United States
North Haven, CT
20 May 2023

36798290R00114